HOW TO BE A FREEL

In this Series

Other titles in preparation

BE A FREELANCE SECRETARY

Your path to a more rewarding future

Leonie Luzak

MEET MS WILSON...
... SHE'S IN THERE
SOMEWHERE!

How To Books

British Library Cataloguing in Publication Data
A catalogue record for this book is available from the British Library.

First published in 1994 by How To Books Ltd, Plymbridge House, Estover
Road, Plymouth PL6 7PZ, United Kingdom. Tel: (0752) 735251/695745. Fax:
(0752) 695699. Telex: 45635.

Note: The material contained in this book is set out in good faith for general
guidance and no liability can be accepted for loss or expense incurred as a
result of relying in particular circumstances on statements made in the book.
The laws and regulations are complex and liable to change, and readers
should check the current position with the relevant authorities or professional
advisers before making personal arrangements.

Typeset by PDQ Typesetting, Stoke-on-Trent
Printed and bound by BPC Wheatons Ltd, Exeter.

Contents

List of Illustrations

Preface

I have eleven years' secretarial experience. I started as an office junior in 1982 with no office or trade skills, became a senior secretary in 1985 and by 1988 was working as a systems administrator.

I became a freelance in 1989 and have been making a living from it since. It is hard work, particularly given the added burden of recession, but the rewards of hard work and careful planning have been phenomenal.

In this book I am passing on the tactics and methods of approach that I adopted and which have secured me a comfortable living. I can give you the tips, but it is for you to work out the volume of work you want or have time to undertake. You will need to establish your own personal commitments and weigh them against the amount of time and patience you are prepared to devote to business.

When I first undertook to make freelancing a business, I changed my way of thinking. Until that point I had always assumed that without an agent, the prospects of building up enough clients were limited. The reason that I believed this to be the case was that I thought that I would be able to secure only long-term contracts, which would account for a large proportion of the work that I received in any given year. I thought that if I received an offer for a long-term contract straight away, I would take it and it would therefore exclude me from building up relationships with other firms. I began to realise that it was not necessary to take on a long-term contract for the purpose of securing the immediate future, and that, if success was going to be attained, I had to restructure my thinking. I had to think long term rather than short term and ask myself fundamental questions about what the possibilities were for thinking long term within the business I had chosen.

When I first mentioned these ideas to my friends, they thought I had gone mad. At the time the country was in recession and I had quite a secure job. The economic climate did not improve in the first year, the second or the third, and to make matters worse one of my initial target areas, the surveying profession, was suffering the knock-on effects of the collapse in the property market.

How and why did it work for me? It was really very simple. I adopted an approach to secretarial freelancing that looked at it as a *business*, not just a job. Throughout this book, you will see and learn exactly how to make a substantial income by using this approach.

A lot of soothsayers and prophets of doom will tell you that it can't be done on a long-term basis, but that is simply because the approach to freelancing by many people in the past has not been businesslike.

The premise to remember is that from being a good temporary secretary, contracting out through an agency and accepting a low rate of pay because you are working through an agent, it is really a very short and uncomplicated step to contracting out your services direct to a company at a price which undercuts the agent and raises your level of income.

Initially, it is not so much a matter of very hard work in the physical sense but doing your research properly within the region that you aim to target. And even then you have little to lose, because if you are experiencing a slump through your own contacts, you can still take on contracts through a secretarial recruitment agency to tide you over.

With good organisation skills, flexibility, common sense (which you are sure to have if you are a good secretary) and a pleasant and obliging personality, a new and rewarding life can be yours. In this book I have tried to cover all the aspects of start up, approach, endeavour, pitfalls, research and selling to show you the way in which you can determine your own future and your own achievements.

Leonie Luzak

1
Checklists for Getting Started

'You are not the same people who left that station
Or who will arrive at any terminus
While the narrowing rails slide together behind you.'

T. S. Eliot

ARE YOU A GOOD SECRETARY?

A senior secretary's job is usually very pressurised. She is normally expected to produce yesterday's urgent report and letters for signature out of one hand, a cup of coffee from the other, and her boss's diary arrangements, travel needs, itineraries, meeting timetables and agendas from somewhere about her person at the drop of a hat! If she happens to speak another language as well so that her boss looks good when that German business associate drops in for a fleeting visit, all well and good — all of which will go largely unrecognised in financial terms.

A normal day's work

If you are a good secretary and you have additional skills, such as a second language, shorthand, a degree in English or whatever your particular skills are, you will be able to capitalise on this as a freelance – ie you will be able to command a price for your service!

WHAT HAVE YOU GOT TO LOSE?

Often the most simple ideas based on very little capital outlay can earn the most rewards. Stop and consider for a moment. Are you currently a temporary secretary working through an agency? Ask yourself why you should not be able to establish contacts and work for yourself. You think it is too difficult? I would suggest otherwise, and the purpose of this book is to show you how simple it is.

There is an element of risk to freelancing, as with everything, but it is for you to determine the proportion of the risks that you take at the outset. If you are cautious by nature, this is an advantage. You will plan more thoroughly, and planning in any business is fundamental for success. In large businesses, and even in medium-size firms, there are people who are employed simply to plan.

BEING AWARE OF THE FUTURE

Consider carefully the employment market in general: not just the employment market of today, but the future employment needs that you assess your area of expertise is going to have. To be successful as a freelance secretary, you must start to consider yourself as a commodity that a client wishes to buy — the more you can offer, the more likely you are to succeed.

Questions you will need to ask yourself at the outset are:

- What can I offer?

- What are my skills?

- How can I service companies in the area where I live?

- What growth potential is there in my area?

- What are my limitations?

- What are the limitations of the area that I want to service?

- Am I a good communicator?

These may seem like very fundamental questions, but appraisal of your qualities, aspirations, type of service and type of working environment are extremely important.

The future is an all-important factor in making an important decision. When you take out life insurance, or a pension, you consider your future. You should do the same in business. Before you start, ask yourself:

- What do I want the business to do for me?

- How much money do I want to make?

- How much will my industry change in the next ten years?

- How will working patterns change over the next ten years?

The last question is particularly relevant. Stop and consider technology just for a moment. Office technology is racing ahead while the world tries to keep pace. This has its advantages for the freelance secretary. The more knowledge you have of systems and their development, the more you can turn your hand from **word processing** to **desk top publishing**, or **spreadsheet** management or a host of different environments to be found on today's **personal computer** (PC) systems, the more you will be establishing your competence in the marketplace.

MOTIVATING YOURSELF

Motivation is one of the most important aspects of everything that you do. This is particularly so in a difficult economic climate where the emphasis is going to be placed on those with a number of skills to offer. Without motivation, enthusiasm and a true enjoyment of what you do, there is little chance of success.

It is very important to draw up an appraisal of your personality and what motivates you – an absolutely honest and frank list of your strengths and weaknesses. There are a number of key factors in adapting your personality to the business you are entering into. Draw up a question and answer sheet similar to the one in figure 1.

Requirement of business	Answer
1. Can you motivate yourself as well as motivating others?	
2. Are you an introvert or an extrovert and will you be able to moderate either extreme?	
3. Do you have the ability to sell yourself?	
4. How good are your communication skills?	
5. Are you flexible enough to mix with all types of people in different environments?	
6. Are you a good manager?	
7. Are you able to work well under pressure within a group and equally able to pressurise yourself into working well on your own?	
8. What are your organisational skills?	
9. How will you react if things don't work immediately?	
10. Are you patient or impatient?	

Fig. 1. Character assessment sheet. Try out these questions on yourself and see how you assess your personality for working as a freelance.

The list of questions is simply a guideline and there are many other question and answer tables that you can draw up and many different ways of doing it. You can apply the same technique as to approaching **cashflows**. If you are naturally good at money management then you will not need rigid budgets and rigid guidelines because it will come naturally to you. If it is not one of your strongest points, then devote a fair proportion of time to writing cashflows and work on your weaker points.

There is a potentially lucrative income in the gaping void of the market for professional freelances. While some of these exercises may seem trivial, they really will help you realise your potential to take some of that income.

Aim to balance your weaknesses and your strengths to make them work for you. Self-awareness is a fundamental asset. Awareness of what you are capable of achieving, as well as what you can't, is a real aid to running your business successfully.

One of the key factors in difficult economic times, or in any period where you are required to be a manager, is motivation. If you are not strongly motivated to do what you do, it will come across to others. Motivation is the key to business success. Motivation brings the confidence to grow and the rewards that come from broadening your skills. Freelancing can offer opportunities to meet people from all walks of life and build worthwhile relationships through offering a knowledgeable service. Awareness on every level, whether it be market knowledge, awareness of your own strengths and weaknesses, specialist skills, money management and market determination, will all help you in getting motivated and building confidence.

KEEPING IN TOUCH WITH RECRUITMENT AGENCIES

Many secretaries, in common with other professionals, have either sought permanent work from or taken on temporary assignments for recruitment agencies. The common reason for using an agent is the established network of contacts which most of them have.

Smaller agencies thrive by linking up on a network basis to provide each other with staff or jobs. They charge each other a percentage of the work contracted out. The larger agencies have no need to adopt this practice because they usually network their own branches within towns and cities. They have large **databases** to draw upon and substantial resources of staff and client contacts.

Traditionally, a secretary is dependent upon her or his agency to fix prices for temporary work and to negotiate annual salaries for permanent work. There is no opportunity for personal negotiation with the agent, even less with temporary work.

It is for all of these reasons that a secretary has come to view a recruitment agency much as a customer at a bank views the bank manager. There is something about recruitment agencies that suggests that they are doing you, the temp, a favour. A secretary tends to forget that it is she or he who is providing the service and that the agency can only establish a name on the quality of the staff it places. Without good secretaries or administrative staff it could not maintain its business. Neither could the bank perform in its business without lending you money – so long as you pay it back!

```
Secretary              MIDDLEMAN
FREELANCE  ⟷  Recruitment Agent  ⟷  CLIENT COMPANY
```

Fig. 2. Cut the middleman out.

If you are undertaking a temporary assignment for a recruitment agency, you are receiving a percentage of what the agent receives for finding you the work, but the real leg-work is being done by you, the temporary. If you work hard and the client is pleased with your work, you are not only providing a good source of income to the agent, you are promoting their work for free as well. Pay should never be considered as gratitude for a favour granted, but payment for services rendered. It is an important aspect to remember and it will help you in thinking flexibly about contracting out not only directly to a client, but in how you deal with agencies if you need them.

It is surprisingly easy to build up your own contacts from the outset and to set your own fees for the work you do by direct negotiation. It does pay, however, to:

- maintain a good relationship with at least one agency, as you may occasionally need fill-in work

- keep your options open

- *never* poach a client from an agency. This is bad ethics and will reflect poorly on you. In any case, you should have no need to canvass business in this way.

Treat the use of agencies much like any other business approach. They need you as much as you need them and if you are good at what you do, they *will* need you. If you start to get into the dirty tricks department then you are cutting off a source of income which may be useful. While you should be aware that you will be taking a drop in rate whenever you use an agency if you have established a good client list for certain parts of the year, you will not mind that drop if it is on a short-term basis and it gives you a security net.

You will need to do a little research, however, into the paying policies of recruitment agencies. You will perhaps find that some of the smaller agencies might not be able to pay you as a company but can pay you on a freelance basis, and some of the larger agencies will only pay you as a freelance if you are a **limited company**. This is enlarged upon in chapter 6 and you should be careful to find out about submitting invoices for payment and how they will be settled, before deciding on the agency that you use.

CASE STUDIES

This section introduces three fictional freelances whose fortunes we will follow throughout this book. Each secretary approaches setting up as a freelance in a different way and we will observe the results of their individual efforts.

Juanita Malette

Juanita Malette is a shorthand secretary who has been a personal assistant to the chairman of a UK corporation for the last ten years. She is in her mid-thirties and her life has revolved around the requirements of the chairman since she joined the company. She has become increasingly frustrated with his temper, his workload and his delegation of everything to her for no reward and infrequent and low pay rises.

Although she speaks two languages, English and Spanish, and is an excellent shorthand secretary, she is not quite sure what direction her skills can be directed in. She has some word processing skills, but only on the system used in her office. She has not really followed technology in the marketplace, as she has not needed to, and feels confident that when she is ready she will be able to secure a more skilled and involved job.

For the time being, she resigns her position with her firm, preferring to sign on with an agency and temp, until she has considered what she wishes to do. While she is temping she decides upon becoming a freelance.

Jenny Anglesea

Jenny Anglesea has few formal qualifications, having left school at 16 (she is now 23) and gone straight into the word processing department of a large legal firm in London. After two years in the word processing department she was promoted to work for two assistant solicitors. Two years later she became a partners' secretary, a job which she has been doing now for six months.

She has become a reliable and efficient secretary and has taken advantage of the in-house courses on desk top publishing, database use and a basic shorthand course. She now realises she has outgrown the job that she does, but isn't confident of securing a better position for herself because of her lack of qualifications. The firm has been through a bad couple of years, owing to the recession, and she has just been informed that she is to be made redundant. Luckily she has some money saved. She decides not to look for a permanent job and after being told by an agency that they can't pay her very much per hour, she takes on a temporary assignment to 'tide her over' and thinks about the possibilities of freelancing.

Suzi Jenson

Suzi Jenson has moved around a lot in her working life. She started as an office junior when she was 21 and has had a variety of jobs over the past nine years. Companies she has worked for have specialised in property development, marketing, scientific research, law and surveying.

She has an A level standard education and has grown with the computing market, particularly as she has changed jobs so many times. In between jobs she has temped with various agencies who have put her on courses for various word processing **packages** and now she is familiar with most of the best selling office word processing software on the market. In her last job she was a systems administrator. She is very adaptable and enjoys changing between environments and as a consequence she is proficient at switching between one word processing package and another.

She has recently come to realise that she is happiest when 'on the move' and has decided to become a professional freelance secretary.

SUMMARY

- Agencies need you more than you need them.

- Start to think of yourself as marketable.

- Put a price on your head.

- Start out on your own terms.

- Channel your energy into positive action.

- Think about your skills and abilities.

DISCUSSION POINTS

1. You have worked out that there is scope for a freelance secretary in your area but not in the field you are accustomed to working in. How do you react to this, and why?

2. You are temping with a recruitment agency in your area that wants to give you a booking for the next six months. The 'but' is they want to give you the booking but seeing as they are offering you this 'chance' they would like to pay you less per hour for it. How do you react to this? Do you see this as a good offer? What would be your considerations before you said yes or no?

3. You are a good communicator and have no trouble with working with a variety of people, but you are unsure of how you would cope pressurising yourself to look for work. What do you do?

2
Equipment You Will Need

THE PERSONAL COMPUTER AND BASIC COMPUTER KNOWLEDGE

Your work as a secretary is without doubt going to involve you in working on a computer. This is mainly going to be for word processing, but may well include work on databases, spreadsheets, desk top publishing, and maybe even accounts packages. If you are coming back on to the job market after several years' absence, it is imperative that you update your skills to learn how to use a computer in the office. Your local technical college will run suitable courses. Private companies will advertise in the *Yellow Pages*, but these will be expensive. See also the section entitled 'Useful Addresses' at the back of this book.

Don't be just an operator of a machine; try to understand a little about how the machine is working. It will give you a good insight into troubleshooting as well as provide you with a sound background in general **systems management**. Most software/**hardware** houses run, or can tell you where to enquire for, systems management courses, and any of the well-established manufacturers operate the same kinds of courses. It is a question of finding the best course for you. Having said this, some software houses primarily provide systems dedicated to their own software, and this means that their equipment is basically not compatible with the vast range of other computers that are available on the market today.

You should learn the difference between dedicated wordprocessing systems and personal computer usage. You should become familiar with operating, say, two or three different wordprocessing packages on one computer and familiarise yourself with the software available for different markets.

By knowing what type of wordprocessing software is likely to be found within which kind of business environments, you have an advantage when approaching your target areas for work, in being able to work out what will be successful and what will not. For example, the legal profession calls on its wordprocessing/secretarial staff to type out long contractual documents which sometimes run into hundreds of pages. Therefore, an advantage of using a system like WordPerfect or **ICL Officepower** is that there is a function available on both packages for automatic paragraph numbering. By inserting a number at the beginning of each new paragraph or sub-paragraph by using a function key, rather than typing it in manually, if there are later clauses and paragraphs that have to be removed/added, the system then automatically changes the numbering through the document when the clause is added/deleted. Obviously, then, any system that has abilities of this nature, is going to be favoured by law firms, when they are considering the purchase of new computer systems and software packages.

Getting started

You will probably be acquainted with word processing systems, personal computers and software packages when you read this book. However, as a guide to the use and purchase of word processing equipment, this chapter includes a very basic introduction to the personal computer, printers and software.

If all you intend doing at home is your own administration, then a computer with word processing facilities will be useful but not essential. If you are intending to work from home as well as in the offices of your clients – and doing so is recommended to ensure the success of your business – then a computer is vital.

A PC is a sophisticated machine which is inoperational until it has programs loaded on to it to make it functional. It has storage capacity ready for its anticipated use and will operate according to the instructions it is given by programs.

It can be extremely confusing, prior to using or purchasing a personal computer, differentiating between hardware, software (the terminology alone frightens many first time users) and the many functions that software can perform on a PC. The confusion arises, as in most professions or businesses, from the use of jargon words. The computer world has developed its own language to guide its functionaries around its everyday use. However, most computer terms and functions can be expressed quite simply.

Computer memory

If you are intending to purchase a PC for working on at home there will be certain criteria that you should look into before the purchase. For example, will there be enough memory for the tasks that you plan to do on it? It is as well to bear the future in mind; it is particularly important to take into account the amount of memory the programs that you intend to install will take up. Some programs, such as spreadsheet software like **Excel**, take up a considerable memory space. If you were considering purchasing Excel and running it alongside word processing and desk top publishing software retaining all three programs resident in the memory, you will need to ensure that you have ample space to do so, remembering the extra amount of memory you will need in order to add your own files and documents.

Plan ahead and make a clear decision as to what you will want your PC to do for you, not only this year, but in years to come. Tell your dealer what you intend doing on your computer, and what your future requirements might be – he or she should be able to advise you. If the advice is not forthcoming or satisfactory go elsewhere.

Many standard computers come with high storage capacity these days which will provide ample memory. You will need to check though when you are consulting a dealer prior to purchase. It is advisable not to buy anything with **disk memory** of less than 80 to 120 **megabytes**. With careful disk administration, you should never run out of storage capacity.

Check what you are getting

A dealer may offer a proposed purchase at what seems to be an exceptionally cheap price, but check for reasons why it is so cheap. There are a host of computer magazines that review PCs in their monthly issues, providing detailed information on price, model, capability, problem areas and general manufacturing information. Do some research before buying a computer and software.

Buying secondhand

Unless you are very familiar with computer systems, trying to save money by buying a secondhand PC is not recommended. You will not know the history of it, what condition the hard disk is in – if the hard disk is cracked it will cost a good deal to put it right; you will not necessarily be able to get a support service as most recognised retailers are understandably reluctant to offer a maintenance contract on a machine whose history they do not know. Another problem, if purchasing at auction, is that you will not know if the previous owner was possibly an insolvent company and whether the machine was under lease agreement. If so, it could mean that the PC can be reclaimed by the leasing company if it was not fully paid for.

WHAT DOES THE TERMINOLOGY MEAN?

There are many types of computer available on the market today and a host of firms that deal in and supply parts for any number of different makes and models.

Whilst the external operation and appearances may vary, all computers are made operational by the installation of an **operating system** which is software written to enable computer start up and is generally termed as DOS (Disk Operating System).

Personal Computers

Once DOS has been installed, the PC is ready to perform functions in accordance with the specifications of the manufacturer's design. Certain PCs are designed with different performance requirements in mind; for example the Apple Macintosh was designed with the primary use of the manipulation of highly developed graphics in mind. The IBM Corporation, for example, were the world leaders in computer design, manufacture and software development until the mid to late eighties. When Alan Sugar introduced the Amstrad he started the rush for the home computer at an affordable price: simplified technology in accordance with specially designed software and run by diskettes not compatible with IBM or IBM compatible machines. Other manufacturers such as AES, Wordplex and Wang developed machines purely for text manipulation and to be used only in this capacity in the office environment. The difficulty with these systems is that they were left behind when PC development in networking and the running of multi-tasks from one PC was introduced. They were limited in their capabilities and are now virtually non-existent with the exception of Wang.

Windows and mouse

Most PCs now conveniently come with highly developed applications as part of the selling price. The development by the Microsoft Corporation of their **Windows** application has been enormously popular; it enables PC users to choose quickly from programs loaded on their hard disk from menus displayed in a series of windows that can be opened and closed by the use of an external **mouse**. The mouse is a hand held device attached to the back of the PC. By rotating the mouse the on-screen pointer can be directed to the operation required and, by clicking on or off, perform a function easily.

It is certainly true that Windows enhances the user's ability to perform tasks quickly and efficiently as it eliminates many of the original keystrokes that were necessary to access applications stored on the hard disk.

Floppy disks

These come in two physical sizes: 3 ½ inch and 5 ¼ inch. The 3 ½ inch size is becoming the more common size. These also come in various storage capacity sizes, usually 360K, 720K, of 1.44Mb (which has twice the storage capacity of a 720K disk). They are used for backing up what is on the hard disk, or for copying information to put on to another computer.

It is very important that you back up all the documents you create. At least copy all documents created in a day on to a floppy disk at the end of the day. That way, if you accidentally delete a file on the hard disk or something goes wrong with the computer, you will not have lost hours of work. It is very easy not to bother with backing up, but it is a vitally important habit to get into.

Floppy disks are slotted into disk drives in the computer casing, normally termed 'A' or 'B'.

Networks

In an office environment you might come across terminals (a screen with a keyboard) which are networked together to run off a central computer. When you buy a computer for home use, this will be known as a stand alone PC.

Modem

You may find that you gain a client who gives you increasing amounts of work to be typed on your premises. It may prove cost effective in this event if you are able to link into their system via a modem communication line, which uses telephone lines to transmit data. This is similar to dialling a telephone number or a fax number, the only difference being that you are communicating from your computer to a host computer in the firm that you are dialling to. If you are receiving

```
C:> - DOS
   - WINDOWS -  ADMIN
           -  GAMES
           -  EXCEL
           -  WORDPERFECT - LETTERS        \ bank
                                           \ client a
                                           \ client b
                       - INVOICES          \ client a
                                           \ client b
                                           \ client c
                       - MAILSHOT          \ SOLICITORS - letter
                                                       - list
                                           \ ACCOUNTANT - letter
                                                        - list
                                           \ SURVEYORS  - letter
                                                        - list
   - HARVARD GRAPHICS/

   - WORD FOR WINDOWS
```

Fig. 3. Example directory structure.

a lot of work from one particular client, you can carry out the work on your premises, and rather than having to take it back for checking and toing and froing from the client's premises – you can send it direct to the firm or even to the firm's printer for proofreading and checking, and it can be amended or sorted out on their premises. This is something for the future, but well worth looking into.

Hayes are the leading company in modem design and development in the UK and they will be happy to provide information on modems if you write to them (for their address see 'Useful Addresses' section at the end of this book).

The advantages of modem link for your own personal usage are various. This stretches from being able to run your bank account by linking into your branch's database, to linking into latest software development updates in America from a worldwide club called Shareware.

Optical character reading (OCR)

One of the modern-day developments is the OCR – optical character reader. By 'reading' texts from books, magazines and all manner of written material with a **scanner**, the scanned pages can be sent from the OCR to a word processing system for use, manipulation, editing and so on. It is a useful and quick method, saving time in retyping of text originating from elsewhere.

However, there are flaws in the system. Unless the OCR is a state of the art machine you may find that if the text you are processing through the scanner is unclear or faded in any way, the scanner will not read the text properly, making characters such as 'd' into 't' or vice versa, or 'o' into 'u', and so on. Scanned documents therefore, have to be carefully checked to make sure they have copied properly.

Scanners are very useful for copying diagrams and pictures into computers – providing you have software that can deal with graphics.

BUYING A SOFTWARE PACKAGE

This is really a question of shopping around. It is important to emphasise that you *do not need to spend a lot of money* to secure a good-quality purchase. A good basic PC, printer and word processing package will be more than adequate. Again, when considering the purchase of software for word processing, take into consideration which word processing packages offer the best functions for your particular use. You should bear in mind that most of today's word processing software comes incorporating spell checking, thesaurus, facilities for line drawing, column making, sophisticated page formatting and text manipulation.

Research word processing programs by reading reviews in magazines, speaking to clients or friends who are already using various programs, and reading the manufacturers' literature. You may find that you need a specialist program, for example, for accounts typing. There are many different word processing packages, but ones commonly used for everyday word processing in many offices are: WordPerfect, Microsoft Word and WordStar (each of which has a version for use with Windows), ICL Officepower, Wang and IBM Displaywrite packages.

BUYING A PRINTER

There are a host of printers on the market, and as with a PC, you can spend as much or as little as you care to. It is important to think of the future when making your purchase. What are your likely needs going to be next to your present needs? Do consider the expansion of your business and go for tried and tested names where possible. As with PCs, printers are continually being upgraded and higher performance models are continually appearing on the market. Do some price comparisons. For example, while it may appear cheaper to purchase a daisy wheel printer for, say, £300, look at the costs at the cheaper end of the laser printer market – a cheap laser printer can cost as little as £600 or £700.

Establish your likely usage and requirements. If you are going to be doing a lot of presentation work or desk top publishing, you will almost certainly need a high performance printer – it would not be cost effective to buy a printer that processes information between PC and printer very slowly. This is a good lesson in cash management. Cash management is not simply about making a purchase within your budget, but securing a purchase from which you will obtain the best possible usage and a long life.

Dot matrix printers
A dot matrix printer is probably the most basic of printers. It produces characters on the page by a series of dots from a print head through a ribbon. It has limited capacity for typestyles, and usually prints in 15, 12 or 10 pitch only. The print quality is poor

and, for a secretary, where the emphasis is on presentation, would not suffice for the type of output you will require. The output is slow and very noisy.

Price: £100 – £150.

Thermal printers

Thermal printers produce a reasonable quality print, but again there are limitations on print style and size of print. However, if a thermal printer is your choice it will service you efficiently in so far as letters, mailmerging and general chart work is concerned. Ribbon replacements and parts are not cheap and the life expectancy with heavy-duty work is in the region of five years. It is a quiet printer.

Price: £200 – £350

Daisy wheel printers

A daisy wheel produces typewritten work, much like on a typewriter itself, by the use of a daisy wheel which impresses the paper with the printed character. The output is slow, but the print quality is good if, again, limited in typestyles and size. Daisy wheel printers often need to be purchased with a special 'hood' to reduce noise levels because they are extremely loud in operation.

Price: £100 – £280

PCs can talk to one another.

Ink jet printers

The ink jet printer is quiet in operation and functions by an ink cartridge which in effect 'throws' the ink character on to the paper. Eight pages a minute and colour ink jet printers can be purchased at a modest sum and there are a variety of typestyles and sizes available. They are a perfectly reasonable purchase for use in a heavy-duty capacity or for limited work and the price, considering their capability, is very reasonable.

Price: £350 – £1,000

Laser

Laser technology has developed since the mid 1980s, and the choices now available in laser printers is wide-ranging. They operate by laser heat thus transferring the processed word to the page, using the same sort of technology as a photocopier. The speed of processing whether it be for word processing, desk top publishing or spreadsheets is excellent (four or eight pages per minute) and the versatility of print styles and typefaces are virtually limitless. The typestyles available are usually downloaded through what is known as a font cartridge (sometimes purchased separately, sometimes as part of the package) which slots into the printer enabling the printer to read from it when the particular styles in the font cartridge purchased are required. Basic model lasers (four pages per minute) are now readily available on the market for a very reasonable price. You will need to replace the toner cartridges (roughly every 5,000 sheets), as with a photocopier.

Price: £600 – £5,000
Font cartridges: £120 – £160

OTHER EQUIPMENT YOU WILL NEED

You need not invest much money until you are sure of what kind of response you are going to receive to your marketing.

It will also be a good idea to research first what kind of markets you are aiming to target, which is discussed in more detail in chapter 3. For example, if you are intending to set yourself up primarily as a legal audio secretary, and you want to gain a high percentage of work at home as well as contracting out your services, then you will need some basic audio equipment.

Audio equipment

Audio equipment, much like PCs, printers and word processing packages, come in a price range. Again, you don't need to spend vast amounts of money. You can find local stationery suppliers to provide you with a perfectly good reconditioned Philips mini-cassette model audio machine, which is fairly standard in the UK, for as little as £80 to £90. However, it may be the case that the types of market you want to approach will use specialised audio equipment. Therefore, first establish what kind of equipment you are likely to need before purchase.

There are models for Sony tape transcription – the mini-cassettes are slightly smaller than the Philips cassette; also Grundig tape transcription machines which are commonly used by the legal profession.

You may find that your client will lend you a transcription machine, so look into this before spending money on what might be the wrong machine.

Answering machine

An answering machine is an absolute must. It is worth spending just that little bit more on one owing to the fact that you will need a quality product which enables you to pick up calls with a pager from any given location. You should not have to spend more than £100 to £120 on this and a good stationery supplier or high street outlet will be able to provide a suitable machine for you.

It is also worth noting that British Telecom provide a number of call-back services now and also ways to divert your telephone to any number where you are likely to be. Advice is available on the services from any of their sales offices for your local area (find the number in the phone book). There is usually a quarterly rental charge for such a service.

Facsimile machine

This may not be something you will want to consider in the first year of trading. Equally, you may secure work with a company that gives you a fair proportion of work at home which requires considerable re-drafting before it is completed. If and when this happens, you may want to purchase a reasonably priced fax machine to enable checking of work before completion without the need for your going to and from the client's premises. This is something you will have to consider in relation to your budget.

Photocopier

Whether you need a photocopier will depend very much on:

- how much work you do from home

- how easy it is for you to use a bureau.

It is not a purchase (or lease) that you need rush into, and experience (and level of frustration at not having one) will help you make your decision at a later date. But it is something to keep in mind.

If at some stage you do need to get a photocopier, spend some time researching what is on the market. It is easy to be seduced by the myriad of functions available on photocopiers these days and as many office copiers have many facilities it is tempting to think you will need these too. But you are likely to need only a very basic copier, and on the probably rare occasions you do need extra facilities, you can get your copies done at a high street print shop. You may want to look into a lease purchase agreement which enables you to pay for the photocopier over a number of years, usually between 3 to 7 years with an option to purchase at the expiry of its lease term. Any reputable dealer will be able to supply details of types of lease agreements.

LETTERHEAD/BUSINESS CARDS

You will need a businesslike letterhead and it is a good idea for professional credibility to have a business card printed. It does not need to be highly sophisticated and if you intend to purchase desktop publishing software, you will be able to design and print your own. The disadvantage in doing this is that your letterhead will be without colour (unless you have a colour printer). You will not need to spend a lot of money on designing a fairly basic letterhead, which should have the name of your service, your address and telephone number.

Your letterhead is important because it will be representative of you. The letterhead in itself can be simple but it should be professional and concisely detail your service. You would probably be surprised at the number of freelances who simply send a 'scrap of paper' to companies with their name and address on and a line stating that they are looking for work. If you send in something like that to a firm, it will go in the bin.

If you are sloppy, people will judge that as representative of your work. If you are well organised and have a professional approach, people will take an interest in you and your résumé, and will be prepared to pay your price. So, the letterhead is important and well worth the capital outlay. You want something professional but not too elaborate that will impress the reader and make them remember you, as well as set you apart from those 'scraps of paper' that keep arriving on the personnel manager's desk.

SUMMARY

Checklist for PC and software purchase

- Ask suppliers and retail outlets for as much information as you feel you need before purchase. Also buy any of the high street PC magazines, most of which provide reviews of PCs and software, prices, and problem areas.

- When you have decided on the make of PC you are considering purchasing, ring up the manufacturer and ask for a list of registered dealers in your area. It's well worth doing as it means you can go to a reputable outlet, approved by the manufacturer.

- When purchasing, make sure you also have a maintenance contract for at least a year for your new PC. Check how much this will cost you per annum. Do shop around. There are varying offers and the market is an extremely competitive one.

- Make sure, when installing, that the engineer checks off with you that he has installed all the parts and software that you purchased. If you are not happy with the installation or find a performance problem after installation, don't be afraid to return to the outlet where you purchased the PC, to get them to put it right.

- Find out if there is a software support line for the word processing software you have purchased. Most reputable dealers in software have their own in-house support service for a nominal fee per annum. You may find this invaluable when you come across a problem that you can't deal with by looking at the manuals.

- Research what type of PC and software will be best capable of serving your needs.

- Don't buy a secondhand PC of which you don't know the history.

- Don't buy a PC without a maintenance contract.

- Don't buy a PC from a foreign supplier unless there is a UK outlet for the product. If you do, you may find there is no support in this country for it, and parts are unobtainable in the event that there is a failing in the system.

- Don't be pressurised by PC sales people. They like to talk in jargon to confuse the lay person. Take your time and do some research yourself. Keep asking questions until you really understand.

Checklist for purchase of a printer

- If you do not purchase your printer from the same retailer as the computer, check with the outlet that they will provide you with the correct cables to link your PC to the printer.

- Research the kind of printer you need, eg if you intend to take on a high content of graphics/art work, you will need a high performance printer capable of outputting these tasks.

- If you are in doubt about what sort of printer you need, consult one of the major manufacturers, such as Hewlett-Packard, who will be able to assist you.

- As with the PC purchase, once you have decided on the type of printer you want to purchase, ring up the manufacturer and ask for a list of registered dealers within your area.

- Remember: a printer needs ribbons or toner cartridges or ink cartridges, and so on, to be of use. Shop around for the best offer from a stationery supplier. You may be able to combine your printing needs with other stationery you will need – envelopes, paper, sellotape, paper clips, and so on. It is well worth having a supplier in your area who is reliable and has a good stock of equipment and stationery.

  You will need to keep a stock of printing essentials – you don't want to find yourself working on a Sunday and suddenly find your ribbon/toner cartridge/ink cartridge has run out and you have nothing to print with and no means of getting anything until the next day! Mail order suppliers are a useful way of purchasing your stationery and computer needs. See the addresses in the 'Useful Addresses' section of this book.

- If you are going to purchase a laser printer, many stationery suppliers and computer firms offer recycled cartridges at cheap prices – as little as £35 to £45. Toner cartridges are not cheap, but they are long-lasting.

- Remember that font cartridges are not usually provided with a laser printer on purchase. You should check, before purchasing a laser printer, what cartridges are available and consider the different typestyles you are likely to need before selecting one or two for the relevant use.

  Unless you buy a multi-purpose font cartridge which will be very expensive, the typestyles found on different cartridges are often specified for either portrait or landscape use. This means that if you purchase a cartridge for standard portrait typing with styles such as Helvetica and Times Roman, you will not be able to get these typefaces if you are producing landscape work until you buy a separate font for landscape printing.

  Do check before purchase what is going to be the best buy for your requirements. Cartridges usually cost in the region of £75 to £95. For a multi-purpose cartridge which prints all styles in either portrait or landscape you will normally have to pay in the region of £250 to £300.

Other supplies

- Negotiate on prices with your local stationery supplier. Take into consideration the firm's reliability; it is as important as the prices the firm charges.

- Visit your local printer to discuss your letterhead requirements. Printers have colour charts to assist in mixing and matching colours, which will be helpful when determining the design and style of your letterhead. The printer will also be able to advise you on the weight of paper – what will be most cost effective and still look professional. If you have a laser printer the paper feeder will not like constant use of thick paper being fed through, so check that the type of paper you want will be suitable for laser printing.

- Try to open an account with your stationery supplier for your stationery needs. You will be invoiced monthly for any supplies that you have had during the preceding month. It is easier to pay a bill by post once a month than to find the cash each time a delivery is made.

3
How to Sell Yourself

WHAT ARE YOU GOING TO CHARGE?

Important aspects of any business are:

- knowing the marketplace

- knowing your worth and how to secure its price

- being aware of what skills you can offer within which environment

- knowing what kind of service you are aiming to provide

- directing your talents/skill/business to the most profitable areas.

Your prices for your work will therefore vary according to a number of factors:

- what area you are in

- what you can offer

- the market rates

- the competition.

You may have to vary your rate to clients according to the type of client you are approaching and what skills you are offering. For example, if you are based in London and approaching West End and City solicitors as a legal secretary and using state-of-the-art word processing equipment, such as ICL Officepower you will be able to up the price because you are applying specialist skills within a specialised market. However, if market conditions are unfavourable, you will have to modify the price accordingly. In a recession, this balancing skill is particularly important. Better to keep the prices within reason and secure work for now; when economic conditions are more favourable and you are still serving a particular company, they will have no objection to your raising your charges.

However, if a company is changing over to new equipment only recently available on the market, then the number of temporary secretaries who can use it is limited. By investing in training, you are therefore able to approach a select market and your services will be in demand. You will then have a niche corner of the market and you can capitalise on this by demanding a higher rate, recession or not. By doing this, you could be securing yourself work for months to come.

Modifying your price structure is something you will have to learn to do efficiently according to the environments in which you will be offering service. Obviously, a frequently used system or an unspecialised market will not call for much knowledge and you will have to lower your rates. If you don't, recruitment agencies and other freelances will have the edge on you – no matter how fast or efficient you are.

Researching the rates
Do some research on:

- The rates that recruitment agencies are charging their clients and adopt a price structure accordingly.

- Find out what sort of agency is charging what sort of rates for what skills to what type of companies.

- Compare rates between different sectors, eg charge rates for a legal audio secretary next to charge rates for a copy/audio typist in banks/hospitals, and so on.

- Find out which professions require specialised terminology and what prices the agencies charge for this.

- Think about comparison rates between work undertaken on the client's premises and what rate you can set for in-house work.

BEFORE YOU START

Keeping a track of what you have offered

As it is important to be flexible enough to lower or raise your rates, it is equally important to know who you approach and what 'hat' you are wearing when you approach them. As you start to research the market, write to different companies, and build up records, you will find it necessary to build up a proper filing structure and lists of who you have written to and what charges you have adopted for that particular target area. With each mailshot that you do, keep a list of who you have written to with a copy of the relevant résumé that you sent with that letter to that particular group of companies (see later in this chapter for suggestions on how to write letters and résumés). If you do not keep records organised and you have an enquiry, you will not be able to go to the file and look up what rate you offered and what you said in what particular letter.

Building on what you already know

Never approach a market with which you are unfamiliar unless you think you can adapt and pick up the relevant knowledge and terminology very quickly. For example, it is no good approaching the medical profession if you have never worked in it. You will struggle with the terminology and it will reflect poorly on you. Leave it to those who have a knowledge of that field.

The right approach to clients

Business success, whether large or small scale, is a matter of being able to support and exploit your knowledge, having a well-organised system and being able to approach people in the right way, putting across to them your depth of skills without overkill. A good approach letter, to the point and well laid out, will bring rewards. Being pushy will not bring good results. You will have to come to terms with waiting, watching and listening to what others have to say. If you are good at what you do and you write to enough people, you will achieve success. Be truthful. Success comes through sticking within the parameters of your knowledge and being able to use knowledge on the client's premises. Beyond that, you don't need to sell yourself. Substantiation of your original letter is enough and it will ensure your service being asked for again.

Adaptability is a key ingredient of success in freelancing. Without it, you will not be able to switch between firms, people and equipment. It is possible to be flexible, but firm. Remember that being a secretary is, essentially, a low profile job. It is a support service. As a secretary, you are the accommodator not the accommodated. This holds true whether you work for yourself or not. If you adopt an accommodating stance, but take a firm hand with regard to running your affairs, you will manage the balance well.

Knowing your own capabilities, and what you expect from your endeavours, will help you in your initial research.

Questions you should be asking yourself are:

- How do I get started?

- What should my contact point be in a firm?

- Shall I write only to large firms, or small firms as well?

- How will I keep in work all the year round?

The next part of this chapter is devoted to discussing these questions.

HOW TO GET STARTED

Get started by writing lists. First, write a list of what your skills are, how you can capitalise on them and what price you can expect for them. Then make a list of the types of firms that you would be able to approach with your skills and delete those that you feel you do not want to work for. If you are not sure what types of professions/ companies fall into what categories, use a local *Yellow Pages*. The *Yellow Pages* is very useful in that it establishes in groups types of companies, as well as listing alphabetically local firms/companies within that group.

When you first start out, approach more than one type of business. Write to two or three related or even unrelated fields to open up your options.

You should choose which types of business to offer your services according to your skills. Choose, say, three fields which are within your experience. For example, if you choose accountancy, you should have some familiarity with accounting terminology. Once you have decided on the three types of firms that you want to service, think about the balance of chance contracts and fixed contracts that you can determine between the three. If you do this, you stand a good chance of success. Work on the premise of knowledge, ie knowing the slack periods within different types of firms. If you choose three unrelated fields to target, it is likely that they will suffer slack periods but, and this is a big but, *at different times of the year*.

Example

Medicine	Architecture	Retail/department stores
Property	Hoteliers	Engineering
Banking	Surveying	Research
Oil companies	Accountancy	Publishing
Marketing	Law	Insurance
Estate agents	Photography	Printer/lithography
Telecommunications	Translators	Insolvency practitioners

If, for example, your initial target areas are to be the legal, accounting and surveying professions, then put aside from your list the other types of companies and target your initial research, interest and prospect letters around the three you have chosen.

You have established what scale of prices you are going to be able to charge and you have three professions/firms that you are going to approach.

PLOTTING THE AREA FOR YOUR INITIAL MAILSHOT

Purchase a map of your local area. Let us assume for the purpose of this example that it is inner London. It is important, in a large city, to focus not on all the areas within the city, but start by picking three or four areas, or postal districts to approach to 'test the water'.

Circle the areas that you feel you can service efficiently and that are easily accessible to you. It is very important to pick a wide circle in the area that you want to target and stick to it. Work through it methodically.

Say you are a legal secretary, living in central London and starting to prepare your target list. Most central London postcodes are easily accessible to you and there is a great source of potential income in central London. It is important, however, to remember as a legal secretary that most law firms are based in WC1, WC2, EC1, EC2, EC3 and EC4. Your other target firms are accountants and surveyors. The majority of the accountancy firms are based in the

West End, though are represented fairly well in the City also. Again, surveyors have a wide representation in both the City and the West End.

Therefore, to win business, your target areas should initially be W1, WC1, WC2, EC1, EC2, EC3 and EC4. You could start by writing to EC1 and EC2, then in your second mailshot, write to EC3 and EC4 companies and so on.

The important thing in targeting is to aim to service the areas which house the businesses you wish to serve, and which you can easily travel to and from.

WHAT SHOULD YOUR CONTACT POINT BE IN A FIRM?

Within commercial organisations and companies, there are often several levels of answerability when it comes to recruitment, staff management and the taking on of temporary help of various natures. In professional firms, there is usually a managing partner who deals with this side of the business. Regardless of this, all of these types of responsibility come under the heading of personnel and, therefore, it is both safest and simplest to address all correspondence to the personnel manager. It will be guaranteed to arrive at the right desk and be read by the right person. If you are working from a telephone directory of your area then it is the easiest way to address a prospective business letter.

There are countless information manuals with reference information on many different companies and professions within the UK. Often these manuals include regional breakdowns. Different organisations, professions and companies use different referencing directories to list themselves in, according to the nature of their business and how much exposure they wish to the general public. To do your mailshot and to be more precise about who you address your letter to, you can buy a host of publications providing information on the companies you may wish to write to. Again, you can spend as much or as little on this as suits you, but in my experience it is much easier at this stage to simply write to the personnel manager using a local business telephone directory.

You don't need to expend vast sums of money when you are 'testing the water'. It may be that you target all the companies within one area that you want to write to and a proportion of the companies are not practising any more. They may have relocated and if this is the case you are likely to have your letter returned by the new occupier of the office or by the Post Office. Delete them from your **prospect list**.

However, if you do want to go into detail and perhaps build up a database, by selecting any comprehensive reference book for your region you should be able to build up an accurate assessment of predominant types of companies and their size. You can then make an assessment of what will be most valuable to you. Make sure you get the latest and most up-to-date version, and if necessary, await publication of the current year's book/manual in order to be sure you are getting the very latest listing of companies practising in your region. You really don't want to work from an old office copy only to find that you are wasting valuable time in writing to companies that simply don't exist any more.

TARGETING LARGE FIRMS OR SMALL FIRMS

The point of mailshots and targeting a field within a region is never to be discriminatory about size or appearance. *Kompass*, for example, produce a Regional Sales Guide each year providing a listing of all companies within a region, giving the size of and the number of employees in each company. A small company does not mean an insolvent or unsuccessful company. Some companies will appear to be very small, but look at the annual turnover. Discrimination can lead to unnecessary loss of business. The company could be a one-person set up that would like you to come in on a Saturday for three hours every week, or it could be a contract with a larger firm for a short period with long-reaching results, or a medium-sized firm for a one-off booking. The important thing to remember with any mailshot is that it could be the first or last letter or any one of the letters in between which secure you work. It is a random method of approaching companies and therefore the results cannot be determined simply by looking at the size of a firm or even at its annual revenue.

The point is, and it cannot be emphasised too strongly, that every opportunity to produce a fixed annual income should be strongly grasped. A fixed contract that expands through one year into another is a good base on which to build. In simple terms, it means that contracts which recur regularly each year are going to support you successfully regardless of the slack periods. Armed at the beginning of the year with these types of contract, you are starting to secure your income. It is therefore impossible at the outset of a mailshot to judge which will be a good firm to write to and which will not – all of them should be approached, large and small. Always remember, large is not necessarily lucrative and that work can and does come from the most unexpected sources.

So far as work at home is concerned, many companies are cautious about sending out their work for typing. They will most definitely want to get to know you first and establish your trustworthiness and reliability. This comes with time, but it is important to be aware of this at the outset to enable you to judge the kind of response you are going to get and to make any calculations about foreseen income that you might expect per, say, every hundred letters in a target area.

The legal profession, for example, has a long tradition in very large firms of making sure that they have an in-house float team. These are very much like temporaries but they temp only within the firm and are paid an annual salary. They do this primarily for economic reasons and another important reason is that it is more secure for the company. Therefore, when you start to write your prospect letters, take factors such as this into consideration and make estimates of what type of response you can expect to receive and for what periods of the year. You will start to get a rough idea of your likely peaks and troughs.

If you are serious in your intentions, it is this foundation at the beginning that will enable you to start building up a regular client base on which you will be able to expand from year to year.

YOUR LETTER OF APPROACH

Shopkeepers can sell only what is on their shelves. They know exactly what market they are selling to in their area and they make their bulk purchases based on the average passing trade that they receive in any one week. In a sense they are lucky because, by and large, they simply sit and wait for the customer to come to them.

As a freelance you are selling experience and skills. You are selling yourself and the process is constant. You cannot afford to write to one batch of companies and then sit and wait for the telephone to ring. You must be persistent with your approaches. And it is vitally important to remember that the initial letter and successful response, are the *beginning* of the sell, not the end. When working as a freelance you are under the microscope and the pressure is on you to maintain high standards. If you are aware of this factor, you

"PLEASE LEAVE A MESSAGE AFTER
THE TONE. I AM NOT ABLE TO
ANSWER THE PHONE RIGHT NOW
BECAUSE I AM WRITING A SALES
LETTER TO GET PEOPLE TO RING ME... BEEP!

will be well thought of, because you will always be performing at your best. This is where the selling really starts and is the determining factor in building up long-lasting relations with the firms that you do business with.

It is important to be aware of this before you write your prospect letter. Remember that everything you write down is what you will have to be able to do if requested. Think about the professions that pay good money and the skills that are required to earn that money. The law is traditionally one of the top earners for a secretary and if you are not a legal secretary, why not look into it? There is now established an Institute of Legal Secretaries in London, and they will be able to point you in the right direction for training.

The more skills you can offer, the more doors you will open up for yourself. Remember the balance of old and new technology because to achieve a high work ratio you will have to switch between the two. Concentrate and focus on these aspects. They are important. Very often the size of the firm, or type of work it does, simply doesn't warrant the expense of changes to newer systems so you will have to acquaint yourself with some of the older systems.

Bolts from the blue

Your prospect letter may sit in a personnel department's filing cabinet for anything up to two years without your even knowing about it. You may suddenly receive a telephone call enquiring about your services out of the blue. It happens. Therefore, much of what you eventually achieve will be in the initial letter and what is rooted in it. It won't have a chance of sitting there for that long if it is:

- poorly presented

- has spelling mistakes in it

- looks shoddy.

It will go into a filing cabinet of another sort – the bin!

Building credibility

Establishing credibility takes time. You will know how good you are at what you do and what you can sell. You may, however, lack confidence. Stick to it and never claim to know something you do not; you will be appreciated and greatly respected for integrity and confidence will come as you build up your contacts. You might find it possible to attend a short course on personal development at a local college of education or training.

Bearing this in mind, work through each list within each area methodically and be direct in your letter of approach. Get your basic letter right at the beginning and you will be able to store it on your word processor and use it again and again to sell yourself. *Spend time at the beginning in getting it right*. If you get it right, you will receive a healthy response and save yourself a lot of time on revision work later on. At this point it is essential to emphasise the importance of a marketing letter and the way in which it is written. While styles are and should be highly individual, introductory letters should:

- be precise

- be courteous

- be professional and businesslike

- outline your fields of experience

- list your skills.

Figure 4 shows an example of an introductory letter. The text in square brackets would be tailored to the individual. The letter should be on a properly printed letterhead (see chapter 2).

You will see from the example letter that

- The first paragraph starts by stating what the writer does and her reason for writing is short and to the point.

- The second paragraph deals with availability. Note that not once in the example letter is the word 'home' used. It is not businesslike and should not be used in a business letter. Companies seem to have an aversion to the world 'home typist' – they imagine, often quite wrongly, the writer is just trying to earn 'pin money' and is not properly established and organised.

- The third paragraph briefly states the writer's experience and expertise (which should be enlarged upon in the résumé). The fourth paragraph underlines capabilities and lists the equipment at the writer's disposal.

- The final paragraph expresses a willingness to meet with the addressee. This is important. It is reassuring for the prospective client company and it shows a preparedness to be flexible. If you are invited for a preliminary interview, you, on your part, can assess the company and begin a constructive relationship with the person with whom you will be dealing.

When approaching specialist companies you should include within your résumé, or letter, your fields of experience within the profession. If you are, say, a legal secretary, it is no good saying you have conveyancing experience when you don't You will undoubtedly be found out and are likely to do your business a lot of harm.

As indicated in the last paragraph you will need to prepare a résumé of your skills. Again, keep it simple and to the point. Put your charges per hour on it. It is important to list everything of relevance on the résumé. It enables the prospective client to see at a glance whether you can be of use to their company and if your rates fit in with their budget for administration. They will respect you for getting to the point. It is an 'at a glance fact sheet' which the client can put in the drawer and keep safely for future use. Set it out on a continuation sheet from your letterhead. Aim to present your résumé in the same professional manner as your letter.

A down to earth approach to what you are selling and good presentation will bring rewards. When you are selling yourself, it is

[Date]

The Personnel Manager
[merge company names and address lists here]

Dear Sir/Madam

I am a freelance secretary [operating as a sole trader] [set up as a Limited Company] and I am writing to you offering my services in this capacity as and when you have the requirement for a typing service or temporary secretarial help rather than your using a secretarial recruitment agency.

I am available Monday to Friday during statutory office hours, or evenings and weekends and am central to most [region – ie London, Manchester, Birmingham etc.] areas.

My background is in [Legal], [Surveying] and [Accounting] terminology which has given me a broad base for other fields,which include [tape transcription work], [statutory audio work], [typing of scientific documents], as well as day to day general correspondence.

Apart from assignments undertaken at my client's premises, I also undertake [specialist work which, in the past, has included compiling a book from tape transcriptions; an international arbitration from C90 tapes and technical brochures]. I have an [IBM and/or Apple Mac systems, with several word-processing packages], [laser printing], plus [specialised and statutory Audio equipment].

Set out on the attached sheet a brief résumé of my skills, my qualifications and my charges per hour and I would be delighted to hear from you if I can be of service to your company.

Yours faithfully,

A. Another
Enc.

Fig. 4. Example standard introductory letter.

important not to get bogged down in long explanations, or provide too much detail. If you are a freelance secretary, this is the topic you are dealing with and this is what any prospective client will want information on. It is my experience from many years of reading CVs and letters of application for jobs that people give too much 'surrounding' detail. What will interest a future client, much like a future employer, is the facts and abilities and how you can assist them. Figure 5 shows an example of a résumé.

Be precise about your service. It may be the case in general commercial companies that you do not need to be specialised in any particular field but, for example, if you are interested in approaching the banking profession and you have experience in corporate banking, mention it in your initial letter of approach.

KEEPING TO THE POINT

Knowledge of your sector or sectors is a valuable asset and this is why it is important to spend a great deal of time on your target area planning who to approach before you actually start to prepare your address lists for mailshots.

Using key words
You will see from the example letter in figure 5 that key words are:

- freelance secretary

- available

- transport

- brief résumé [of my skills, my qualifications and my charges per hour].

These words and ultimate sentences are important and so is the order in which they come. Any prospective client is basically interested in:

- What your service is and how can you help the company.

A. ANOTHER - FREELANCE SECRETARY

Nationality: [   ]

Charge Rates Per Hour: [WP/Audio   £11.00 per hour
                             WP/Copy   £10.40 per hour
                             Copy/Audio WP Sec £11.40 per hour]

Secretarial Experience: [ ] years working experience
                             in London [Birmingham/Stoke-on-Trent]

Secretarial Fields of Experience:

                             [SURVEYING] -   PARTNER LEVEL
                             [LEGAL]   -   PARTNER LEVEL
                             [ACCOUNTANCY] -   PARTNER LEVEL

Secretarial Skills:

Wordprocessing:	[IBM	-	Displaywrite 3 & 4
		-	Wordperfect 4, 5 and 5.1
		-	Wordstar 2000 V. 4, 5 & 6
		-	Wordplex
		-	Multimate
		-	Microsoft Word
	ICL	-	Officepower
	APPLE MAC	-	Microsoft Word
	AES	-	Plus and Superplus
	WANG	-	OIS, VS5, VS6 and VS65 Officewriter
	OLIVETTI	-	Wordstar 3 & 4]
Typing Speeds:	[Copy	-	90 w.p.m.
	Audio	-	90 w.p.m.]

Fig. 5. This is an example résumé. You should aim to cover as many skills and your charges on this sheet to give the client an at a glance fact sheet which he/she can keep on file.
[ ] – square brackets are to give you an example of listing your skills to the full, you will need to state your own particular fields of experience, skills and machinery that you use.

49

- Your availability and how that fits in with the company.

- How mobile you are.

- What skills you have and what are you going to charge for using them.

Give the client these answers in the body of your letter and on your résumé without rambling.

Never:
- Send a handwritten note to a firm and expect them to reply.

- Write a letter without attaching a résumé. A prospective client wants to know what you are capable of doing before he or she thinks about seeing you. Consider: would you buy a car from a salesman without seeing the car first? No! So don't expect the client to take you on trust, or without any information about you.

DEALING WITH ENQUIRIES

Your answering machine

As mentioned in chapter 2, an answering machine will reward your investment time and time gain, so invest in something that is going to be reliable. Ideally, it should be a model that includes a pager, to help you pick up your calls when you are away from home. (If you have done everything correctly, you will be away from home a lot!)

Look after your machine – for example, keep the tape heads clean so that the messages are clearly reproduced. It will be disastrous for your outgoing message to be fuzzy and unclear because the tape starts to get dirty or it cuts your message in half.

Aside from the presentation of your letter, and before the prospective client has seen you, the most important selling feature to you is what they hear on the answering machine if you are not at home to take their call. Think about your message carefully before you record it. Spend as much time on it as you need, but practise recording a message something along the following lines.

'Hello, this is [who you are], and thank you for calling. I am not available to take your call at the moment but if you would like to leave a message, *I do pick up my message every hour and will call you back as soon as possible.* Please leave your name, your telephone number and the purpose of your call after you hear the tone. Thank you for calling.'

Recording a message is an individual matter and will be a question of what you feel comfortable with. Your message should, however, contain one key ingredient, the same one which will run from your answering machine right through to the service you provide and you build up your relationships with others: that is *reassurance.* You will note that the words 'I do pick up my messages every hour and will call you back as soon as possible' are picked out in italics. Why? For the very reason of reassurance. You are reassuring the caller that you are reliable and are going to contact them. When people who need a support service telephone that service, it is usually because their needs are immediate. By saying that you pick up your messages every hour you are giving an assurance that that immediate need will be responded to within at most that time. People will wait for an hour and will be impressed when you stick to it, and *do* stick to it, because your reputation can be built up or spoiled extremely quickly on this factor alone.

The reliability factor

If you make a study of people responsible for administration in businesses, you will notice a common factor. That factor is the worry of being let down. There is a natural worry that the person whose services they are considering using may be unreliable or unsound in their knowledge. This book places a lot of emphasis on the importance of sincerity, integrity and professional standards. This is because the knowledge that has gone into writing it comes from years of experience on both sides of the fence, as a user and a provider of a service. Without doubt, the appreciation of first-class work and a professional approach translates into a guaranteed income.

Just as it is important that you can provide the service that you say you can, there are many other considerations that will attract a prospective client to feel that they can depend on you. So make sure that feeling of reassurance comes across in your answering machine message and your telephone conversations.

Following up on enquiries

When you follow up an enquiry from a prospective client, try to adopt certain procedures. As a matter of routine, find out as much about a company as you can for your own records. When you telephone, even if you are unable to assist the company because you are unavailable at the time it needs you ask about the nature of the work required, the type and size of firm it is, the type of word processing software they use and about what their future requirements may be.

Find out the position of the person who called you (ie is he or she a secretary, a manager, a personnel officer). You will know their name already as they will have left it on the answering machine. If it is not an immediate need that the client has – for example, the personnel manager may be planning summer holiday requirements – arrange an appointment to go and see him or her. Even if you can't undertake the particular contract you are being asked about you should aim to try and arrange an appointment. You have nothing to lose but the time it takes for a brief meeting and it is well worth it in trying to establish a rapport with someone you may be working with in the future.

Using what you have found out

When you return home, type up a file note on your meeting, or even if you don't have an appointment, you should type up as much information as you can ascertain on the company – where they are located, how to get there, what they do, and so on – as you may need to have it quickly to hand at a later stage (see chapter 5). You can always learn so much by meeting and negotiating with other people. The trick to master is working in the present and managing your present needs, with one eye to the future and the possibilities which lie ahead. So do take an interest even if it does not result in anything more than an interested enquiry. You never know.

Most people like to feel that *you are interested in them*, so take a genuine interest. Leave discussions or negotiations about hourly rates to the end of the conversation. Particularly find out about the number of support staff that the company has, as it will give you an idea of how much work you might receive in the future. Let people tell you about themselves. Encourage this because it is an important facet of working with anyone in any job. It is not only about being good at what you do but about investing in other people.

Adjusting your rates

Once a meeting is established and a satisfactory interview has taken place, you can then bring up the subject of your hourly rates. It is enough just to ask if they are satisfactory. Of course, they are happy with the prices or they wouldn't have called you in in the first place, but it is not only for this reason that you should be enquiring. You might be able to find out how your charges compare to that of agencies that have approached the client, or other freelances. Sometimes, you might find you are exactly on a par with the prices of agencies, sometimes a bit below and if you are specialising on a contract, slightly above. It is a good idea to build up a file on how you compare in your particular market, as it will give you a guide to your approach over money and levels of income that you can expect to receive. You also need to establish that you are selling yourself at the right sort of market rate and you can only do this properly by gentle enquiry.

CASE STUDIES

Juanita Malette

Juanita Malette has written an excellent letter of approach, having decided to target marketing and publishing companies in her area. On browsing through the *Yellow Pages* she has discovered that there are 150 of these companies within the areas that she feels she can service. She thinks that this is a lot of companies to write to. She is aware that her résumé is a bit 'thin' on technical skills as she has knowledge only of the one word processing system. She sets her charge rates, however, above the local recruitment agency that she has occasionally been using for placement. She has not put her language skills down on her résumé. After writing to the publishing and marketing companies she wonders how many of them will use the word processing system she knows and whether she should have perhaps upgraded her word processing skills before approaching companies. 'Oh, I'll always be alright – I'm a good secretary – I'll always get something,' she thinks to herself.

She receives only three positive responses, two stating that they will keep her résumé on file in case the company requires her services and one direct booking for three month's time. She receives a further ten replies stating that her word processing experience does not match the software that that firm uses.

Juanita should have looked into upgrading her skills, even if only by one further software package, to open up possibilities of work. Taking things for granted, however good you are, will not bring about success. She should have summarised her language abilities on her résumé and included a pricing structure for translation work. As well as writing too few letters, she should also have written offering her services to a third group of firms which specialise in translation or languages work.

Jenny Anglesea

Jenny Anglesea has got herself well organised. She has done a fair bit of research of the sort of companies which are prospering in her local area. Being a legal secretary, she has already prepared her target letter for solicitors. She has stated her experience in desk top publishing and data processing on her résumé, and having completed a course in WordPerfect for Windows and Microsoft Works word processing programs adds these skills as well. There are a number of architects practising in her area, but realising the recession has hit the building trade badly she decides to write to them for in-house work only. There are three universities in the city where she lives and she decides to approach them, too.

She is very worried about the recession and does not feel confident to offer her services at a high rate. In the end she adopts the rate that the recruitment agency has been paying her, not differentiating between the shorthand, secretarial and audio skills she has. 'Better to get work at any price than be out of work,' she thinks to herself, although inwardly she knows she is selling herself too cheaply. She receives a large and interest response from the law firms in her area, who are delighted with her skills and rates per hour. She receives only one reply from a local architect, who expresses interest in using her in-house service on occasion, and no response from the universities. She is pleased that she has secured work, but disappointed with the overall response and frustrated at the pricing structure she has adopted.

Although Jenny's approach was correct, she made the mistake of not adopting different pricing strategies for different skills. She has undersold herself. In choosing architects and universities to write to Jenny has approached a market suffering badly from the effects of long-term recession and an exclusive educational environment which will not provide a high turnover of work. Jenny should have chosen a back-up of at least one other profession or industry that could provide her with a fair proportion of work. Her fields of prospecting were too limited.

Suzi Jenson

Suzi Jenson knows exactly what she can do and has planned a detailed list of surveyors, solicitors and accountants to write to. She has put her A level qualifications on her résumé, all her word processing skills and she has carefully worked out what charging structure she is going to adopt for the three different professions. She has drawn up a likely response she can expect from each of them and has written her letters accordingly.

Her highest charges are to the legal profession; they are broken down into audio, copy and secretarial services. She has adopted the same pricing structure for the accountancy companies, lowering her prices by 10% to accommodate the lack of terminology she will be expected to know. In her target letter to surveyors she has shifted the emphasis to a service from her office typing reports and surveys, being aware of the recession, and modifying her prices by a further 5% drop.

She is aiming to secure a balance of work, some in-house fixed contract work at a reduced rate and temporary assignments on the client's premises for a higher rate. Suzi has reckoned that her systems knowledge should bring in a fair proportion of replies as her cross-section of skills will suit most of the word processing packages that the companies in her area are likely to use. Having written over 350 letters, Suzi receives over 30 letters from solicitors, 10 letters from accountants and 15 letters from surveyors in response. Three of the letters have led to contracts on the client's premises and one surveyor has requested her in-house secretarial service.

Suzi has not only thought about ways in which to balance pricing work, but has balanced her approach between different sectors of the business world. She has taken into account slumps in work and possible lucrative income and has written a lot of letters. She has not left anything to chance or struck out any source of income, nor has she limited her horizons.

SUMMARY

- Get to know what businesses are thriving in your area.

- Prepare three letters, each aimed at a different sector of the business world and vary your pricing structure accordingly.

- Prepare a list of the types of firms you would like to service.

- Research locally what the going rate is for a temporary secretary.

- Don't write to a specialised industry in which you have no knowledge.

- Think about your typing/word processing/language/other skills and how you can apply them to freelance work.

- Prepare a résumé incorporating your skills and qualifications.

DISCUSSION POINTS

1. Give an example of poor preparation for a prospect letter.

2. Give an example of good preparation for a prospect letter.

3. What would be an example of good or bad planning in terms of securing work for yourself?

4. A client responds to your letter favourably. It is a client where you can command a higher price for your service because the word processing system is relatively new and few people know how to use it. He offers you an immediate three-month booking if you would be prepared to negotiate over your hourly rate. Do you agree? If so, by what percentage do you agree to drop your hourly rate?

4
Managing Your Contacts

THE NEED FOR EXPERTISE

In today's recessionary climate, expertise is vital in any field of business and it is the key to success for secretarial freelancing. Experience is of paramount importance and training is fundamental to this. Breadth of vision and the confidence to expand your fields of experience can be achieved only by keeping abreast of changes within that field. Because word processing packages and personal computer choices are wide and varied, to keep abreast of upgrades in technology and word processing packages it is helpful to subscribe to institutes which provide newsletters, seminars, training courses and information.

There are a host of magazines available on PCs and word processing packages, and some word processing software companies issue their own magazine to keep users advised of the upgrades they are making. **WordPerfect,** for example, issue their own magazine on a monthly basis which is called *Perfect User.*

There are institutes for secretaries to join such as the Institute of Wordprocessing; and there are specialist institutes, such as the Institute of Legal Secretaries which provides information on word processing and secretarial skills in relation to the legal profession. Many of the large corporations and medium-size firms now have **in-house** 'help desks' and training programmes for their staff.

If you are setting yourself up as an expert on one system in one field, then you will not need to be so adaptable to other training and knowledge on other systems. However, by doing this, you are precluding yourself from a large market of companies and firms who do not operate the system that you are familiar with. It should be remembered there are a high proportion of firms that use old systems or older computers and still run older versions of modern word processing **software**. Some firms still use dedicated word processing systems, although rare now, because to keep abreast of the ever changing technology is not cost efficient, particularly to smaller companies. Larger companies often run more modern software on computers which can be used for multi-purpose tasks. If you can make yourself as familiar with the older computer and word processing packages as you are with the **state-of-the-art technology**, you are anchoring work for yourself in firms where agencies are finding it difficult to place people.

It is therefore of vital importance to remember that the speed with which technology is changing does not filter through to the consumer with nearly the same rapidity. Particularly in a recession, people will 'make do' with their old systems. So while it is important to keep abreast of the multi-purpose skills that are required from today's secretary – which range from audio typing right through to printing spreadsheets and desk top publishing – it is necessary to try to keep a balance of knowledge of older and more dated systems.

Aiming in one direction, with one target in mind will limit your horizons. There are countless freelances who undertook contracts in the late eighties with firms who kept them in long-term contracts that went on into one or even two years. It was a lucrative time and firms were not worried about keeping a 'float-like' temporary in the firm and paying her or him weekly as a freelance. Then, when recession was upon us and the firm made cutbacks, they were the first to go. If you are calling yourself a freelance and taking on contracts like this, you are not really a freelance but at the beck and call of one company, and if they suddenly terminate your contract, you will have nothing to fall back on. If, however, you are prepared to invest in training, be flexible and adaptable to change, you will build up contacts who will call upon you time and time again.

Building up your contacts will depend on:

- your target area

- what kind of service you are aiming to provide

- what kind of industries, professions or services dominate the area in which you aim to service.

If you are a legal secretary, for example, but the area in which you live is predominantly steel manufacturing or heavily geared towards the service industry, it would not be prudent to set yourself up as a freelance legal secretary. You will therefore have to do some considerable research into the type of companies that operate in your region and be adaptable to their requirements.

HOW TO KEEP IN WORK ALL YEAR ROUND

The secret of this lies in your:

- skills

- adaptability

- availability.

The more skills that you are able to offer – and this is again where you will see the importance of training – the more you will be able to turn your hand to almost anything. The difference between you and the next person could be in your adaptability to suit the circumstances of the company that is following up on your letter. The more adaptable you are, the more people will seek your service as someone who is obliging and easy to get along with.

Exploit the need for holiday cover. Once you have had a meeting with a prospective future client, bring them round to the idea of giving you advance warning each year of holiday cover. It does not always work, but you have nothing to lose by asking. Aim to fix your year in terms of contracts. Act as a business person, not a freelance. In your first year you will spend a lot of time establishing contacts, scheduling yourself into new routines and re-ordering your own personal circumstances around the needs of others. A golden rule in this is to be the accommodator. If you want to keep in work and establish new links, always remember you don't know to whom your name is being passed at any time and what will come from each meeting and contract.

It is advisable to never allow yourself to become 'too comfortable' in a contract and too attached to any one firm. If you like and enjoy working at the firm, see it as a bonus for next year and as a place that you can look forward to going back. Never see it as your main source of income and your only contract, otherwise you will be starting to close the door on opportunities that could arise in the future.

Temporary secretaries often feel that making a living from being a freelance offers no prospect of success because they do not understand how you can balance contracts throughout a year. They are approaching the freelance market from the wrong direction and with the wrong aims and goals in mind. If you are approaching a target area with the hope that you will secure a long-term contract, you are approaching it with the wrong attitude.

Keeping a balance

You should be aiming for balance. Stop and think about one in-house contract that brings you in a £100 a week. Turn it into an annual income. It is a base on which to build. One fixed contract can take time to gain, but if on average you obtain one in-house contract a year and aim to build up fixed assignments for holiday cover every year, you are already on the way to securing a substantial salary base from which to cover slack periods.

If your chief aim in writing to a company is the hope that the personnel manager will write back and offer you a six-month booking, you are not approaching freelancing as a business – you are looking for a permanent job without the word 'permanent' attached to it. You are also limiting yourself and freelancing is very much about making, communicating and building up a list of contacts beyond your actual ability to service every single one.

The reasoning behind this is that there must be an aim towards balance. Start adding up your likely return of responses and the amount of forward bookings you can expect to receive next to the regular typing work that comes in locally and you are securing yourself a permanent job. It is unreasonable to start with the expectation that you will definitely be in work all the year round, but if you apportion the income that you make for the large majority of the year, you should be able to provide yourself with a cushion for the slack times.You, at this point will be thinking, 'yes, but most of the holiday cover will only be the summer, surely?' this would be quite wrong.

Example

Stella Midford has four fixed contracts per year which she does without fail. These are for:

- *A firm of surveyors that has one secretary who goes on holiday for two weeks in January each year and two weeks every Easter.*

Stella agrees in year one that she will be happy to fulfil this contract yearly and in her year scheduler and her future planner she makes provision for these four weeks of the year.

- *A firm of accountants that has more than one secretary.* However, Stella is only called in to cover the accounts typing twice a year. Once for two weeks in June of each year and once for two weeks at the end of September. Again, during the course of year one, Stella fulfils the contract and agrees to provide a back-up service on a yearly basis at these times of the year.

- *A commercial company, that employs a legal secretary, who takes her holiday for two weeks in November of each year.* As before, after fulfilling the contract in year one, Stella secures that contract for the succeeding years.

- *A firm of solicitors, that books Stella from July through to the beginning of September to cover in the litigation, company and commercial sections of the firm.* This, again, is an annual requirement.

From the above you will see that gradually Stella is accounting for her year. You will see that this already covers twenty-six weeks of work in any given year which is aside from the fixed contracts that she may coincidentally receive from in-house work. This is what you should be aiming for.

A practical and realistic approach to work with the right aims in mind, can secure you enough contracts to build upon, which will enable you to run a successful business. A vitally important factor in keeping in work all year round is continued promotion of your services. Never allow yourself to be lulled into a false sense of security by work that you are currently undertaking. Keep plugging. Keep writing and keep opening yourself to new experiences. To give you an example, let us assume that you have a contract from March through to the end of June and you feel that you are fairly comfortably off with your cashflows and you are doing well. That is fine, but remember, a letter not written might well be a chance lost not necessarily for the present, but for the future.

On a small scale, your might receive an enquiry asking you if you could do one audio tape a week. If you had stopped writing, you might never have received that enquiry and one audio tape a week is

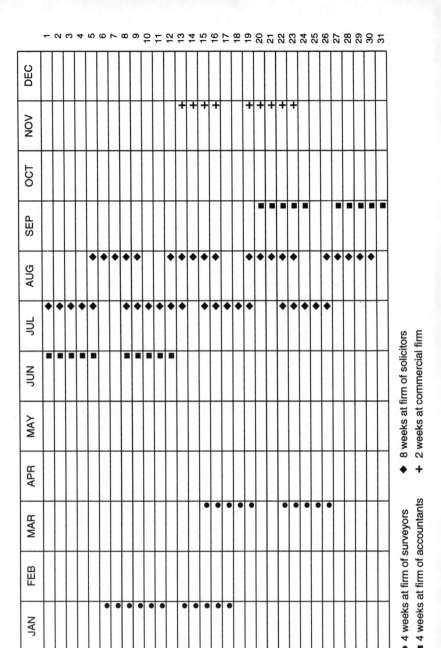

Fig. 6. Planning the year - how Stella Midford plans her contracts
for her various clients.

fixed income. It may be that you might receive a 'future work' enquiry. You may have a personnel manager who would like to meet you in respect of future requirements even if you are not necessarily needed right away. Continued marketing means continuing possibilities. If you don't practise this, it would come to the termination of your fixed contract and you are left without other openings.

When it comes to writing letters, there is no such thing as writing too many, and if you find after a year that you have covered your three original target areas then start thinking about expansion, explore other types of firms that you feel you could service and approach them. There is nothing to lose but the price of postage and your time in preparing a mailshot.

DOUBLE BOOKING

Never renege on an agreement. If you have promised to undertake a contract with one firm for a period in the year, don't go back on your original agreement if a better offer comes up. If you start doing this and it becomes obvious, you will lose respect and, consequently, work. If you make agreements to be at a place on a certain day at a certain time, be there. If you start moving the goalposts, clients will think that if you can cancel one thing that you had previously arranged with another client, you might do it to them. It really is very bad practice.

But don't let an enquiry go without a fight either! If you are out on contract and you receive a call from a client needing cover, ring them up, explain the situation and ask them about the kind of assistance they need, what kind of system they use, how long the contract would be for. Is it a matter of typing which you could do in-house, or do they need someone on the premises? Only by communicating with people can you improve your negotiating skills and find out about their company. So follow everything up. Most people will appreciate the trouble you take in returning their call and the interest that you show. It may incline them to bear you in mind for the future.

Sorting out genuine mistakes
If you do find that you have inadvertently made a mistake and booked two clients in for the same day or week, ring up one or other and make your apologies. Try to ensure that this doesn't happen, because once people feel that they have been let down, they will be

loath to use you again. If it happens that one of the bookings is a new client, go to the older client first. Explain what has happened and state the fact that the other booking is a new booking and that you feel that if you didn't go and work for them you might be losing other work for the future. If you are honest and it is a genuine mistake, they will probably make allowances this time and appreciate you for having told them the truth rather than just 'ringing in sick' or making excuses.

DEALING WITH DISAPPOINTMENTS

This is not easy for anyone. When you are first starting out you feel you are offering a good service for a reasonable price. If you then don't receive more than a handful of responses stating that you are being 'retained on file for future reference', it can be very disconcerting.

However, there are positive aspects in receiving replies at all. If a company is taking the trouble to reply, it shows you have written a good letter. If you had sent a scrap of paper you would not have received that reply and it is even more unlikely that your services would even be considered.

When you approach firms in a professional manner, they will appreciate it but it may be the case that they cannot see how they can use your service at the time that you write. Do not be too disheartened. It happens. A company might reply to you initially stating that they are keeping you on file. You might think this an end to the matter and consider your letter has probably gone in the bin. You may be wrong. They may well keep the letter and contact you a year later. You just will not know, so don't give up writing. You will be both surprised and pleased if they do contact you at a later date, because it means that the quality of your letter and the hours expended on it have not been wasted. While that is not immediate cash in the bank, it is most certainly worthwhile for your future prospects.

You may find at the outset that you receive numerous enquiries about your service and they lead to nothing. It happens, not just in this business but in every business, and a percentage of your prospect letters are going to attract enquiries which lead nowhere. Turn the negative into the positive by making a note of all such enquiries, and you will begin to know what kind of enquiry is going to be fruitless and what will generate a positive reaction.

Patience is an absolute must, and it is true that a little of its goes a long way. You will reap the rewards of your labour, but nothing comes without trial and error, waiting and a great deal of investment in terms of time. If you can stick out the bad times by concentrating on the positive aspects and if you can work hard there will be rewards not only in terms of being able to determine your own income levels, but also in the sense of achievement and satisfaction that comes from working for yourself.

There may be a time when you are undertaking a contract for a client which your client anticipated would take a week. You finish the work on the Wednesday and at the end of the day, the client says that he is really sorry, but considering that there will be nothing for you to do for the Thursday and Friday he will not be needing your services for the rest of the week. This is really infuriating. However, don't lose your temper. You should explain calmly that you have booked the client in for a certain period and turned down other work in order to service this contract. It may not work, but you should try. You should also, firmly and politely, suggest that you will be out of pocket if you are out of work for the remaining two days and would they consider part payment for the lost work. The point is that you should let them know – without losing your temper – that they cannot do this to you again and that you are not a pushover.

CASE STUDIES

Juanita Malette

Sally Fields, senior secretary in a firm of surveyors has rung Juanita to make an appointment to meet with her. She has read her résumé with interest and her boss thought the price was a very reasonable one. Sally is rather forgetful, unfortunately, and on the evening of the interview, her husband has rung her to say that the central heating pipes have exploded. She forgets about the appointment with Juanita, who turns up at 6.00 pm on the dot to find that Sally has left for the day and her appointment has quite evidently been forgotten. A tall, rather odd-looking chap relays this to her. She doesn't know who he is. She doesn't care, she is absolutely livid.

'I came here especially from the West End and it's pouring with rain! I really think it is appalling manners to make an appointment with me and not to be here!'

'Well, I am sorry Miss Ummm? Sorry, what was your name?'

'Oh, really! Nobody even knows my name! It's Miss Malette. I had an appointment with Sally Fields at 6.00 pm.'

'Well I'm sorry Miss Malette, you will simply have to ring Miss Fields in the morning to rearrange the appointment, there's nothing to be done about it now.'

Juanita walks out of the office and goes home, tired and her pride sorely wounded.

The next morning, however, she decides to telephone the firm back again to be met by the frosty voice of Ms Fields. 'I am sorry that I wasn't here, but I was distracted by an emergency at home and I understand you spoke to the senior partner of the firm, who told me you were extremely rude. I am afraid therefore we will not able to use your service. Thank you for calling.'

This is an example of losing your temper before knowing all the circumstances, which can be incredibly damaging. If Juanita had politely said something like, 'Well, I'm sorry Ms Fields isn't here, I'll give her a ring in the morning,' and then lost her temper in the privacy of her own home, she may have still had a possible client the following morning.

Jenny Anglesea

A Mr Snell pops round to Jenny Anglesea's home as he is local to her area and is the friend of a businessman who has received one of Jenny's prospect letters. Mr Snell is considering starting up his own business and thinks that Jenny would be a handy person to know locally for his administrative needs.

Jenny is delighted that she has been recommended and listens for two hours to Mr Snell's dreams and aspirations and how she might fit into the scheme of things. She is anxious about the time as she has other work she has to finish but is too polite to say so. Mr Snell wants to know if Jenny could do the odd letter and perhaps do his postage for him. 'Of course,' he continues, 'when I have my own office, I would be able to offer your considerably more, but do you think you might be able to run off the odd letter for me, for say £2.00 a letter?'

Jenny thinks this is ridiculous and thinks about the hassle of turning on the computer, typing and printing the letter, taking it round to Mr Snell's house, waiting to see if it is correct and, if not, doing the retype and the posting – all for £2.00! However Mr Snell seems so keen and enthusiastic and partly to get rid of him so that she can continue with her work, she agrees to undertake such work.

He leaves, agreeing to come round on the coming Saturday morning with the first letter. The following day, Jenny reorganises her other arrangements to accommodate Mr Snell. However, in the evening he rings and says he is terribly sorry, but could they make it Sunday instead, something has come up. Jenny agrees, wishing she could get out of the contract now, but not liking to upset anyone.

While Jenny is right to consider every opportunity, there are people who are going to fall into the category of time wasters. There are a surprising number of 'Mr Snells' and they invariably cost more than they are actually worth in terms of work. Jenny was not assertive enough. As soon as Mr Snell suggested the £2.00 per letter, she should have said kindly but firmly, 'I'm so sorry Mr Snell, I only contract out on an hourly rate which I can only reduce for bulk regular work. I hope you understand that I am a freelance and any other way of working simply wouldn't be equitable.'

Suzi Jenson
John Derrick of Derrick Dingle & Derrick gives Suzi Jenson a ring after receiving a letter from her about her services.

'Hello Miss Jenson, I have the need for a service such as yours for a few days a week, do you think you could pop in to see me and have a chat about it?'

Suzi agrees an appointment to see Mr Derrick and on the arranged day visits his office. They discuss terms and the word processing equipment but Mr Derrick, who has only been trading for a year, has not yet established his administration requirements.

'How have you been operating up to now?' Suzi asks.

'Well, I've had temps as and when I've needed them. Actually I usually use an agency because it's normally an afternoon or spur of the moment thing – but their charges are so high. I have been thinking about using a freelance who I could call upon as and when, so to speak. Which brings me round to the three days. If I were able to offer your 24 hours work a week but on a phone you when I need you basis, would that be suitable?'

'I understand your predicament and your difficulty in determining your requirements, but I don't think I will be able to help you because an arrangement like this would prevent me from taking any other work. I would, in effect, be an employee waiting for a telephone call, and not free to secure myself any other employment. I hope you understand my situation. However, if your circumstances change and you can give me a more precise indication of your requirements, then I would be happy to assist you.'

Suzi has handled this well. She has been polite but firm. After realising that the contract was a very 'loose' arrangement and not likely to serve her well, she has turned it down. She has the confidence to know that this is not the sort of offer that is going to result in a profitable outcome for her. She quickly extracts herself from involvement, without cutting herself off from a possible source of income if something more tangible is offered.

SUMMARY

- Never renege on an agreement.

- Never take a booking which is going to end up costing you money to undertake.

- Never preclude yourself from work by narrowing your approaches to companies.

- Never be rude to a prospective client, no matter how exasperating the situation.

- Listen before you act.

- If you are in doubt about a contract being offered to you and you don't want to make on the spot decisions, always go home and think about it first.

- Draw up a table of expected response to your mailshot. Break down the expected response in terms of working at home and temporary work on the client's premises. Then produce an estimate of the proportion of the year you are likely to be in work and in what types of firms. (You will be using this information further on in the book to prepare your cashflows.)

- Think of a difficult situation in which you could find yourself with a client and write down your way of dealing with it. Use the case studies above to assist you in preparing this.

DISCUSSION POINTS

1. You have accepted a booking from one client and a further client
   rings you up offering a booking for the same period but for a
   higher hourly rate. What do you do?

2. You were offered a four-week booking and on the Friday before
   the booking, the client rings up to cancel. You are furious. What
   do you do?

3. You are undertaking a booking and the client suddenly says that
   you have completed all the work so quickly that they won't need
   you for the remaining two days of the week? How do you react?

5
How to Organise Yourself

KEEPING RECORDS

We have seen how planning is fundamental to every business. Now we will move on to organisation, something which as a secretary you will already be very much aware of. Your prospect lists are a database and you should think of them as a directory. Keeping them filed properly and updated is vital. You will need to monitor your response next to these lists and if you are not organised, you will start to lose track of the groundwork you have done. Remember, work that you do on preparing your potential contracts is unbillable time, so you need to set up a good system in the beginning to cut down time spent in organising yourself!

Without keeping a record, you will not know what price you have charged which companies and on what date you wrote to them. If you receive a reply, or an enquiry, you will not be able to turn to the file to discuss the contract, because you won't have any information on it. When you write to a wide target area, you will most certainly not be able to remember everyone you wrote to, on what date and on what terms.

Set up an A4 ringbinder and as you merge letters for mailshotting the company addresses into list form including a telephone number, and keep that list within its category in your file.

Keeping up-to-date

When you receive responses from companies which do not actually offer you work but state they are keeping you on file, make sure you note it in your prospect list. Write the date they replied next to their name on the list, and the general content of their letter and then file the letter in the relevant section of the file. Record keeping is vital in building up a picture of what types of companies are responding and in what proportion. It is also important to keep all your letters that are returned to you. Note the reason for failure of delivery of the letter, and mark it off on your list next to the relevant company; if it is a 'gone away' return, cross the company off your list. If you do have slack periods and you want to go through your prospect list, if you have not marked off your responses and your returned letters, you could spend fruitless time phoning companies who have either responded negatively or are no longer located at the address you originally wrote to.

When you start up your prospect list file, you should section it off. For example, say you want to write to accountants, solicitors and surveyors in the London postal areas W1, WC1, WC2, EC1, EC2, EC3, EC4. Your prospect file should be divided along the following lines:

Heading divider	Accountants
Sub-divisions	WC1
	WC2
	W1
	EC1
	EC2
	EC3
	EC4
Heading divider	Solicitors
Sub-divisions	WC1
	WC2
	W1
	EC1
	EC2
	EC3
	EC4
Heading divider	Surveyors
Sub-divisions	WC1
	WC2
	W1
	EC1
	EC2
	EC3
	EC4

Within each section after you first send out the mailshot, you should make a merged list in alphabetical order of all the firms that you have written to and the date on which you did the mailshot. You can then use this as a cross-reference for responses, dead letter returns, and future prospecting. Dead letter returns are letters returned by the post office where:

- the firm has 'gone away'

- the envelope is not addressed properly

- the addressee has refused to accept the letter

- the occupier of the address has marked the envelope 'Not known at this address'.

File your listing to a diskette and file it within the relevant sub-division of your ringbinder. This provides you with a secondary back-up by building up a database. If at any time in the future you need the addresses again, you will have them at your fingertips for use with any further letters you may wish to write. You may start to specialise in a related field. For example, you may acquire additional skills such as shorthand or stenography and need to write again informing your prospective clients of your upgraded skills.

After the first year as a freelance, go through the lists that you originally made and consider writing again to the firm who did not respond to your original mailshot. A year is a suitable time between one approach and another.

USING MASTER PRECEDENTS AND PROFORMAS

Managing your time

With the groundwork established, you should start to think of your time and how to use it most cost-effectively for running your own administrative affairs. For example, cut down the amount of repetitive work that you do. Precedent documents are documents which have been used before and can serve as an example for the future. In other words, masters from which to copy or work. Precedents for documents, faxes, letters, invoices, timesheets and variable information standard documents should be planned at the beginning. If you are going to be invoicing one particular client on a weekly basis for work done, then you do not want to retype the invoice every time you switch your PC on.

In the same way, any other documents which you are going to be typing on a regular basis you will want stored ready for repetitive use. Organise your PC's disk in terms of a filing cabinet, with directories and sub-directories for your client work, your personal correspondence, reports, invoices and timesheets (see chapter 2). Within each of these directories you will want to set up **proforma** documents that you can use regularly. For example, if you have a client for whom you type survey reports, you will need a directory for the client and within it you will want to set up a further directory for surveys. If these reports are typed to a certain layout that the client has requested, you would ideally have a proforma that you can work to each time you type a new report.

Creating standard administrative documents

Creating invoices

Set up a directory for invoices. Create an invoice proforma and once satisfied with it make a copy of it for each client that you will be billing with their name and address on it. In this way, each time that you invoice the client, you will not need to type anything but the hours worked and the amount charged.

With many word processing, spreadsheet and desk top publishing programs a host of proforma documents are now supplied for the user's use. You will need to research this yourself depending on what software you decide to purchase. A lot of software has excellent facilities for 'form merging', which means creating a standard proforma and putting a merge command with the proforma document only where the variable information is likely to change on a regular basis. You might find these time-saving.

You may wish to design your own invoice something along the lines of the one shown in figure 7. It need not necessarily be laid out in this format, but the information must relate to the hours on the timesheet for the work carried out and be sent in with a copy of the timesheet. The timesheet does not have to be elaborate but it must have recorded on it the date the work commenced, the hours worked – segmented into days and a line allocated for the signature of the client and the date it was signed. See figure 8. Whatever your invoice looks like, it should be on your headed paper and should contain the following information:

- the date of the invoice

- the invoice number (this will be the next number in your invoice book – your accountant or a Local Enterprise Agency will be able to advise you on startup bookkeeping for your business – see chapter 6)

- the client's name and address

- what the invoice is for

- the number of hours worked and the hourly rate

- the total amount charged

- your invoice terms eg 'Payment within seven days'.

If you are registered for VAT you will need to include the VAT amount and your VAT registration number (see chapter 6). Take a copy for your copy invoice book. Always keep a copy of your signed timesheet with a copy of the invoice that you are issuing to the client.

Creating timesheets
For work carried out on the client's premises, the timesheet document is a must and the hours produced on it will correlate to the invoice that you later submit. It will be essential for you to produce a timesheet when completing a weekly contract with a firm for the client's signature, as much to protect your own interests as theirs. Once signed, your timesheet is in effect proof of satisfaction of completed work. To operate on a trust basis is unprofessional and provides you with no security. It could be the case that you submit an invoice for payment for a week's work duly completed and find yourself with an unpaid bill and no evidence to suggest that you were ever on the premises!

The timesheet does not have to be elaborate but it must have recorded on it the date the work commenced, the hours worked – segmented into days and a line allocated for the signature of the client and the date it was signed. See figure 9.

Set up a directory in your word processing program for timesheets and keep a proforma timesheet document for each client. When you submit an invoice for services carried out, you

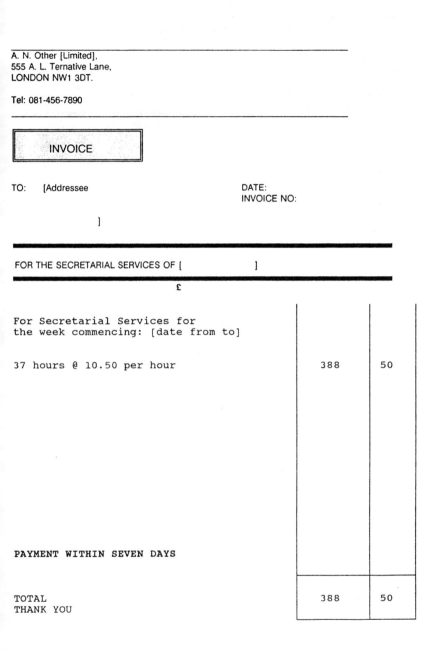

A. N. Other [Limited],
555 A. L. Ternative Lane,
LONDON NW1 3DT.

Tel: 081-456-7890

INVOICE

TO: [Addressee   DATE:
                                           INVOICE NO:

                   ]

FOR THE SECRETARIAL SERVICES OF [   ]

£

```
For Secretarial Services for
the week commencing: [date from to]

37 hours @ 10.50 per hour                   388      50
```

PAYMENT WITHIN SEVEN DAYS

```
TOTAL                                       388      50
THANK YOU
```

Fig. 7. Example invoice.

TIMESHEET

TO: [client: address

        ]

Week Commencing <u>16th March 199-</u>   Total Hours <u>35</u>

	Mon	Tues	Wed	Thurs	Fri	Sat	Sun
A.M.	9.30	9.30	9.30	9.30	9.30		
LUNCH	1	1	1	1	1		
P.M.	5.30	5.30	5.30	5.30	5.30		
TOTAL HOURS	7	7	7	7	7		

Signature of Client _____

Date Signed   _____

Fig. 8. Example timesheet.

A. N. Other [Limited],
555 A. L. Ternative Lane,
LONDON NW1 3DT.

Tel: 081-456-7890

TO: [Addressee: Client

        ]

SCHEDULE OF HOURS WORKED

DATE TYPED	TYPE OF WORK	HOURS
26/10/199–	Arbitration Report	5
28/10/199–	Arbitration Report	6
30/10/199–	Arbitration Report	6
1/11/199–	Arbitration Report Corrections	5

TOTAL HOURS WORKED	22

Fig. 9. Schedule of hours worked.

should attach the original of the timesheet to the bill, keeping a copy filed with the invoice or in a file specifically set up for timesheet records. You will probably find it easier to keep the copy of the signed timesheet with the relevant invoice and then if there is a query, you have to hand the relevant documentation. If you undertake a lot of work for one particular client, you may want to set up a client file in your filing cabinet and keep an extra copy on the file. Therefore, if you needed to look through the records of one particular client in a hurry you would not have to sort through other bills and timesheets until you found each one relevant to that client.

KEEPING A LOG OF IN-HOUSE WORK

Keep a separate A4 sized book for work you do in your own office. You should rule it off in columns under the headings:

Date of work This is important for billing purposes and your own records.

Type of work A short description of the type of work you are doing for the client.

Typist It will be you in the beginning, but have the column there – you may sub-contract and will want to know who did the work for the purpose of checking it when it comes back.

Word processing package used You may have more than one word processing package on your PC so have the column there. Some of your contracts may be considered in-house but you do them on a Saturday at your client's premises using a typewriter – still mark it off as in-house work and use the abbreviation 'TW' or similar.

'Hours from', 'hours to', and total hours' What time you started the work, what time you finished it and the total time spent. This is very valuable as you may be undertaking on-going work and will not be submitting an invoice immediately. When you have finished the work you can use your record book to count the hours in preparation for the final or interim bill.

Client Fill in the name of the client you are doing the work for.

Disk ref This is to help find the work quickly within the directory of the word processing package.

Billed When you have completed the in-house contract and have added up the hours spent, you can then tick it off in the billed column and when you refer to your record book, you will know at a glance what work has been charged and what remains outstanding for invoicing.

Invoicing for work carried out in-house, will not require a timesheet to present to your client, but if you follow guidelines given above you will have an immediate reference for hours worked from which to bill. Translate the information from your log book onto a Schedule of Hours sheet (see figure 9) and attach it to the invoice, clearly showing the hours you have worked, the date on which you undertook the work and what type of work was carried out. Create a directory in your word processing software for in-house hours and within it create a precedent for Schedule of Hours worked.

Faxing

If you intend to purchase a facsimile machine, then do a precedent for faxes that you think you might send regularly. This will save you having to search through your address box for a fax number every time you want to send a fax. See figure 10.

While the methods of setting up standard form documents and precedents may differ from one word processing package to another, the result of setting up precedents is the same. It is time saving and is good organisation.

SETTING UP PRECEDENTS FOR CLIENT WORK

Once you have set up proformas for your own needs, you will be ready to set up the proforma documents that you may need for your client work. Many firms and different professions work to standard documents which in layout are the same every time they are used, but the information in parts of the document is variable. The type of precedents that you create will, of course, depend on which areas of business you have approached. For example, if you have approached accountants, you will have to set up proforma standard accounts documents as accounts documents are all the same, excepting the

FACSIMILE TRANSMISSION

TO: [   ]

ATTENTION OF: [

FROM: [

DATE: [

NO. OF PAGES: [ ]   FAX NO: 071-422-3456

SUBJECT: [variable information]

MESSAGE: [First typing line for message.)

Fig. 11. Facsimile proforma.

variable information that appears in them, i.e. what company the accounts are being prepared for and the annual figures for that company. If a firm of accountants want to give you sets of accounts to type each week, and you are unaware of the best way of doing it on your word processing package, you could spend hours of unnecessary time setting up columns for figures and standard layouts.

The client will expect you to know exactly the best and fastest method of typing their documents – in fact they may at some stage expect you to tell them. If you are using time in developing methods while you are actually doing the contracted work, it is unbillable time. By following these simple guidelines, you will establish clients who will have confidence in your abilities.

In the same way, if you have approached legal firms for litigation typing, you will be setting up precedents for affidavits, lists of documents, index of documents, consent orders, and so on. This can only serve to benefit you because, again, if you are using valuable time in unnecessary typing of headings and titles which always remain the same but for the variable information, then you are in effect losing money.

IT'S FILED UNDER "P"
FOR PRECEDENTS

Creating client directories
Set up directories for your clients. Within these directories make
sub-directories for the work requiring precedents. Once these
precedents are established on your word processing package, run
off a hard copy for your client file – or, alternatively, have a
ringbinder file for 'Master Precedents' – and file a copy away with
the reference typed on it where you have stored it on the word
processor. Thus, if you need to check whether you have a particular
document set up or you cannot remember where you stored it on
your word processing software, you will be able to cross-reference
the file for it.

Remember: you may want to sub-contract at some point in the
future. If you are disorganised and your work is not filed properly
and if precedent documents are not easily accessible, someone else
trying to work for you will lose valuable time in searching for
documents that could be to hand within minutes if you are
organised at the outset. Try to set up simple systems which anyone
could come to and find easy to use. You will be doing yourself a
considerable service if you do.

HOW TO MONITOR YOUR PROGRESS

Run your freelance business professionally. Keep file notes on your
activities and dealings. Write your thoughts down about contracts,
do progress reports, monitor the types of work that you receive and
in what proportion.

Using a wallplanner
Purchase a wall planner and three sets of different colour stickers,
say blue, yellow and red. Use one colour for sticking on the days of
the year that you are in work on clients' premises, the other sticker
for work done at home and the third for days unemployed. Buy a
wall planner that shows the days of each month with the month
heading at the top of the chart. This is so that your week may be
split between two different firms and you should mark the day/days
with the stickers and write next to the sticker the company where
you are going to be working. Use the other colour for days that you
are not in work, and at the end of the year you will have an 'at a
glance' picture of how you have got on. It will show you the weak
and strong periods of the year, and the proportion of work you
received from which companies. You can use this wall planner in

conjunction with your invoice book to prepare **work percentage comparison tables** (see figure 6).

Using a pocket diary

Also purchase a pocket diary to correspond to your wall planner, making sure that the diary has an evening section for each day, so that you can make a note of every evening and weekend contract that you gain. Using your wall planner or diary at the end of the year, you will be able to prepare your analysis of work gained separating the proportion of in-house work from your temporary assignment contracts.

At the end of the first and subsequent years you will be able to analyse your table to monitor performance and make plans for the forthcoming year.

CASE STUDIES

Juanita Malette

Juanita has been extremely busy – sending out prospect letters and rewriting her résumé to include her language skills – and she has received an increasing amount of Spanish translation work at the weekends for a Spanish travel agent that has recently opened up in her area. She is delighted. Things are going well and she has had enquiries regarding her service from a number of firms. Because of the lack of time, she keeps meaning to organise her prospect lists but she just never seems to get around to it. She thinks, 'Oh, I've got it on the word processor somewhere if I need it, but I'm OK at the moment, I'll just write it all down if a new client phones me and check the details later'.

David Brown, personnel manager of a shipping form, Stroydent Shipping, is interested in Juanita's language skills and telephones her leaving a message on her answering machine when he discovers she is not in. It is nearly 5.00 p.m. and he ask Juanita to call him the following day.

Juanita picks up her message before leaving work and is very interested in the contract, and makes a mental note to call Mr Brown in the morning. As soon as she gets in she has some urgent translation work to do and clean forgets the answering machine message and through force of habit wipes the tape before she goes to bed. As she does it she realises what she has done and all she can remember is the name of her caller being David Brown and the company name. She can't remember what type of company it is and under what mailshot she has sent it. Three hours later, after searching through all the mailshots in the word processing directory, she finds the company name, address and telephone number and is able to phone Mr Brown the following day.

If Juanita had organised her prospect lists, she could have saved herself hours of work and searching and got an early night!

Jenny Anglesea

Andy McFergus, the personnel manager of Millson Wilward has received the letter for Jenny. The freelance they have been using over the past three years is about to go on maternity leave, leaving them short of an excellent accounts typist. Andy is interested in Jenny's résumé and sees that although Jenny doesn't seem to have a great deal of accounts typing experience, her résumé and letter are well set out and her charge out rates are very reasonable. He thinks that instead of having Jenny on the premises typing accounts, as the recession has cut back the amount of accounts typing anyway, he will contract the work out to her at home. He gives her a call to see if she is interested in meeting him.

Jenny is delighted to have received the enquiry and goes to see Andy McFergus. He offers her a contract and gives her five long sets of accounts to type asking her when she will be able to return them. Jenny is inwardly horrified at the rows and rows of figures and imagines the column work involved in setting up a precedent. But she promises a two day turnaround and takes the bundle away with her.

On getting home, Jenny realises she's going to have to take the day off from her day contract the following day because it is going to take her some time to set up columns, tabs and rulers to set the accounts out properly. In the event, it takes her four or five hours because some of the accounts are for holding companies and have up to eight columns for figure work. Jenny works through Wednesday evening until the early hours and all day and night Thursday, and finishes the work. Exhausted and with a loss of other work, she return the accounts to Andy who is very pleased with the work and the relationship is established for future work.

Although Jenny has been successful in getting the work and meeting the deadline, she could have achieved the same goals with far less hassle if, before writing to firms of accountants, she had checked the type of work she was likely to receive and set up precedents for accounts typing on her word processor. She would then have had proforma documents to work with as soon as she returned and needn't have given up a day's work with another firm on the Thursday.

Suzi Jenson

Suzi, because of her cross-range of experience on different word processing software has been extremely busy on contract work to various firms. She is starting to receive a great deal of work at home from a local solicitor which she is completing in the evenings. She is working on one such evening on an affidavit for her new client when the telephone rings.

'Hello there, you don't know me but I received your letter a couple of months ago and I am actually quite local to you and think you may be able to assist me. Mr name is Mr Fairchild and I and another partner run a small litigation practice on the High Street – Dingleby & Partners – perhaps you've seen it?'

'Oh yes, I do know it' – while Jenny is talking she takes her mailing lists ringbinder and leafs through to the appropriate list and sees Dingleby & Partners, flipping to the end of the section to refer to the résumé she sent.

'Are your rates still the same?'

'Yes, they are – I see that I specified an in-house typing service – you being located so near by.'

'Yes, that's right – actually that would suit us better as we don't have a word processing system and what with all the long documents, it is becoming impossible for our daytime secretary to type all the correspondence as well as documents for Court and so on ...'

'Well, I think I can help you there. I have precedents set up on my word processor for all standard litigation documents – perhaps you'd like to come and see them and we can discuss how I may be able to assist you?'

They discuss times and Suzi, pleased with the new enquiry, hangs up the telephone.

Suzi has everything well organised. She has her original prospect lists to hand and can quickly look up information on anyone she has written to and she has precedent documents to hand in the event that she needs them.

SUMMARY

- Organise yourself at the outset by setting up proper filing systems and records.

- Always section off different types of companies under different headings for your prospect lists so that you will be able to locate them easily and quickly if needed.

- Once a mailmerge is done, copy all the information lists on to a floppy disk for safe storage, to free your hard disk space on your computer and for ease of access if you need the information again. File the disk with your listing.

- Keep a separate log book for in-house work.

- Set up precedents to work from.

- Always get a timesheet or schedule of hours signed by the client.

DISCUSSION POINTS

1. Give an example of bad organisation and how this could lose you: (a) the client, and (b) money.

2. What would be your idea of getting the maximum opportunity from a situation where a client telephones to enquire about the sort of services you can offer for a small partnership or company?

3. How would you go about explaining what a precedent is to a company which has contracted your services to sort out their typing arrangements and get them generally organised?

6
How to Manage Your Accounts

BASIC BOOKKEEPING

You will probably need to seek some advice on what accounts to keep from an accountant, your bank or a local enterprise agency. If you are intending to set yourself up as a sole trader, the bookwork will not be unduly arduous.

You will need to purchase a **cash book** from any high street stationers, an **invoice book**, a **petty cash book** and two or three A4 ringbinders in which to keep copies of your purchases, bills and your copy invoices.

Keeping a cash book
A cash book is a basic and essential account book which, in simple terms, on its left-hand side records your sales receipts (ie income from your freelance contracts) and on the right-hand side lists your expenditure through the bank. An accountant will advise you in detail on the proper keeping of a cash book, but in principle you use the cash book to record *all* money and cheque transactions. For example, if you issue an invoice to a client for the sum of £120.00, once you have entered it as an invoice in the invoice book, you will enter it in your cash book on the left-hand side giving the client's name, the amount, the date, and the paying in book number when you receive payment. The information in this book should reconcile to your bank statements and as you reconcile them with the cash book, you will tick off each entry as you check it in conjunction with your statement. In exactly the same way, you will list your expenditure. You can set up headings in your cash book appropriate to the expenditure that you are likely to incur. See figure 11.

Left-hand page of cash book:

SALES

Date	Client	Pay in no.	Amount
12/02/93	P. Jarvis	005	120.00
19/02/93	R. Sumi	006	365.00
24/02/93	M. Evans	007	95.00

Right-hand page of cash book:

EXPENDITURE

Chq. no.	Date	Payee	Amount	Stationery	Postage	Telephone
100161	11/02/93	D. J. Office Supplies	36.07	36.07		
100162	14/02/93	BT	201.89			201.89
100163	15/02/93	Smiths	5.64	5.64		
100164	21/02/93	Post Office	36.23		36.23	

Fig. 11. Cash book.

Keeping a fees day book

The fees day book is used to record the amounts of your invoices, to whom issued and on what date. Each time you issue an invoice you should give it an invoice number. Invoice numbers should be sequential. A tip in keeping your fees day book: keep a date paid column and when you receive a cheque for your services, enter the date on which you receive it. A further tip is to leave two or three lines when you reach the bottom of the page to allow space to total off. Alternatively, if you prefer, total off each month under a separate end column so that you will be able to see how much you have made each month at a glance and make comparisons. This will assist you in preparing and monitoring cashflows (see section on cashflows). See figure 12 for an example of a fees day book. You will need a VAT column only if you are registered for VAT, of course (see later). You will note that invoice number 004 is ruled off to indicate the last invoice of the month and extended to the right is the total for the month of March.

Once you have issued your invoices, you should make a copy of them and put a copy in an A4 ringbinder for 'Invoices to clients'. If you are contracting out to a client on their premises, a copy of the signed timesheet should be filed with the invoice for record purposes.

Set up an A4 ringbinder for your purchase invoices. Ideally, the headings that you adopt in your cash book should carry across to your A4 ringbinder. You should section off the ringbinder with standard dividers and as you settle your incoming bills, tick the invoice/bill and write the date you paid, on it. Then file it away under the relevant section. For example, if your purchase was an item of stationery – such as letterheads – file it under stationery once it is paid. You will need to set up a miscellaneous section for the occasional bills that you are unable to categorise.

Handling petty cash

Petty cash is all money expended that does not go directly through the bank. There will be occasions when you purchase such things as pens, lightbulbs and other general items for which you will need to keep receipts. When you do make a purchase with cash, keep the receipt in a box marked 'petty cash'. It is a good idea to keep a small notebook in your petty cash tin in which to list your petty cash items, totalling it off at the end of every month, or so.

Inv. No.	Date	Client	Amount	VAT	Total	Date Paid	Monthly total column
001	20/3/93	A. Blogg Limited	340.00	59.50	399.50	23/04/93	
002	21/3/93	A. Black Plc	240.00	42.00	282.00	12/04/93	
003	25/3/93	Black & Black	23.10	4.04	27.14	29/03/93	
004	30/3/93	A. Blogg Limited	340.00	59.50	399.50	25/04/93	March - £943.10 (net)
005	01/4/93	Biggs & Biggs Plc	212.00	37.10	249.10		

Fig. 12. Fees day book.

CASHFLOWS, PROJECTED INCOME AND CASHFLOW FORECASTING

You may have heard the term **cashflows** and have found it off-putting. It is really very simple and it is exactly as its name suggests, a projection of the flow of cash in and out of a business.

How a cashflow forecast works

An established business will prepare cashflow forecasts according to a number of factors: fixed income, potential income, and expected percentage increase/downturn in income. This information is taken from the invoice book, the sales figures over a given period and the projected sales based on growth/downturn over a fixed period. For example, a company established in 1993 will project cashflows for 1994 based on the income received in 1993 adjusted for any growth or decline experienced during that year, plus the percentage growth/decline it expects to achieve in the following year. The cashflow forecast should take into account the peak sales periods of the year as well as the slump times and an average figure can be produced which is the total turnover for the year or the six month period divided between twelve or six months.

The bottom line

From the figures prepared according the method described above, the overheads and monthly outgoings are then deducted. At the bottom of the cashflow you are left with a cash balance representing cash turnover minus cash outgoings. When the company is healthy there should be a positive balance of turnover minus overheads which forms a cumulative set of figures which steadily increases and becomes your cash balance. A minus figure at the bottom would suggest that your outgoings are more than your income, and you are therefore not earning enough, or have too many overheads. That really is very much of a nutshell description of cashflows and an expert would be able to advise you in more detail, but for the purpose of starting up it is simplest to keep the amount of information on a basic level.

Approaching the bank

If you intend to approach a bank for a fixed loan or flexible overdraft facilities, the bank will need to see a cashflow forecast of your potential income and outgoings. The bank will not even consider lending you money unless it can see evidence of your proposed money management. Your bank manager will not consider you prepared for the business you are undertaking unless you show him or her some concrete evidence of your expectations.

Being realistic

It is important for you to make both pessimistic and optimistic assessments. Prepare two cashflow forecasts – one based on a pessimistic realisation of your targets, and one based on an optimistic realisation. Then prepare an average between the two sets of figures based on your chosen proposed pricing structure between the fields. (As mentioned earlier, you may well have different pricing structures for different types of firms and when calculating cashflows you will need to take these factors into account.) Keep these cashflows to hand, work out what you can live on and how to apportion your expected income over a twelve-month period. Work out your likely busy times and calculate for periods when you anticipate that you will not have any work.

Figures 13 and 14 are two cashflows, one based on a pessimistic forecast of earnings and overheads, and the second based on an optimistic forecast. Figure 15 shows a cashflow which represents a conservative forecast. Study these and prepare some of your own. You will see from the figures that the outgoings are estimated calculations. You will be able to translate these calculations to reflect your own outgoings/expenditure and get a more realistic budget which you can apply in relation to estimated turnover 'minusing' your outgoings which will help you to determine likely profits.

Armed with a set of three such cashflows you will be able to approach the bank with tangible evidence that you have prepared for your business. You should also write a proposal — it does not have to be long-winded — of how you intend to set about establishing yourself and what your long-term goals are. It may be that you are not looking for financial help from the bank, but it does you no harm whatsoever to do this work anyway. There may be a time when you will need to borrow and if you have done the groundwork and are running your business well, you will be looked upon favourably by the bank.

You will also benefit from keeping these cashflows for your own use and you should keep a file dedicated to this. At the end of your first six-month period, measure your actual income next to the income you projected. This will give you invaluable guidelines to forecasting in the future. You will find it beneficial to repeat this exercise at least every six months.

Once experienced in preparing cashflows you will be able to build elements of chance into them, and draw up a budget much like any household budget. Questions you can ask yourself are:

- Have I provided any money for training?

- Have I provided myself with backup for slack periods?

- What will my tax liabilities be and should I be building up a reserve for these liabilities?

- Will I need to buy new equipment in six months' time?

- If I need to sub-contract, what available cash will I have to pay sub-contractors?

These are rudimentary examples, but thinking about them will help you to foresee future possible expenditure. If you don't do these exercises, you may find yourself with sudden and unexpected bills which you will not be able to meet. Also, remember to allow for your living expenditure each month. You won't be any good to anyone if you haven't allowed for buying yourself food!

LIMITED COMPANY OR NOT?

You definitely need to take appropriate professional advice on the question of your business status. However, there are three ways of setting yourself up initially as far as establishing yourself as a business is concerned:

- sole trader

- partnership

- limited company.

You can simply call yourself by your own name (or a business name, if you wish) and establish yourself as a sole-trader, or you can establish yourself as a limited company. Whatever you do, you will

CASHFLOW 1 – A. N. OTHER – Optimistic forecasting – First six months January to June

Based on *full eight hour day contract work* and *15 hours home typing contract work per week.* Contracting out at *legal rates.*
Rates: Legal – £11.50 per hour; Home contract work – £9.50 per hour; Standard secretarial work – £10.50 per hour.

SALES (FREELANCE CONTRACTS)	Jan	Feb	Mar	Apr	May	June	Total
In-house typing contracts	570.00	570.00	570.00	684.00[1]	684.00	684.00	
Legal secretarial contracts (five day week)	1,840.00	1,840.00	1,840.00	1,840.00	1,840.00	1,840.00	
TOTAL CASH RECEIVED	2,410.00	2,410.00	2,410.00	2,524.00	2,524.00	2,524.00	14,802.00
OUTGOINGS/EXPENDITURE[3]							
Mortgage/Rent	300.00	300.00	300.00	300.00	300.00	300.00	
Rates/Council Tax[4]	20.84	20.84	20.84	20.84	20.84	20.84	
Services: Water	13.34	13.34	13.34	13.34	13.34	13.34	
Electricity	23.34	23.34	23.34	23.34	23.34	23.34	
Gas	23.34	23.34	23.34	23.34	23.34	23.34	
Stationery & equipment	35.00	35.00	35.00	35.00	35.00	35.00	
Clothing	100.00	100.00	100.00	100.00	100.00	100.00	
Food	300.00	300.00	300.00	300.00	300.00	300.00	
Travel	40.00	40.00	40.00	40.00	40.00	40.00	
General	120.00	120.00	120.00	120.00	120.00	120.00	
	975.86	975.86	975.86	975.86	975.86	975.86	
TOTAL SALES LESS EXPENDITURE	1434.14	1434.14	1434.14	1548.14	1548.14	1548.14	
TOTAL SALES LESS EXPENDITURE CUM[2]	1,434.14	2,868.28	4,302.42	5,850.56	7,398.70	8,946.84	

1. In the first month of the second quarter you gain a further client who provides you with three further hours per week in-house contract work. Your cashflow will therefore reflect this.
2. Cum is short for cumulative and it means to keep a running total of the total sales less expenditure line to give a figure representing the amount earned in total (in this case the six month period).
3. Based on fictitious figures.
4. Where bills are not issued monthly, take the annual or quarterly charge and break it down into a monthly charge.

Fig. 13. Example of an optimistic cashflow forecast. The figures used are for illustrative purposes only.

CASHFLOW 2 – A. N. OTHER – Pessimistic forecasting – First six months January to June

Based on seven hour day contract work and 6 hours home typing contract work per week commencing only in the second quarter of the period. Contracting out at standard secretarial rates.
Slow growth with only three working weeks in the month. No increase in work in first six months.
Rates: Legal – £11.50 per hour; Home contract work – £9.50 per hour; Standard secretarial work – £10.50 per hour.

	Jan	*Feb*	*Mar*	*Apr*	*May*	*June*	*Total*
SALES (FREELANCE CONTRACTS)							
Home typing contracts	00.00	00.00	00.00	228.00	228.00	228.00	
Standard secretarial contracts (five day week)	1,102.50	1,102.50	1,102.50	1,102.50	1,102.50	1,102.50	
TOTAL CASH RECEIVED	1,102.50	1,102.50	1,102.50	1,330.50	1,330.50	1,330.50	7,299.00
OUTGOINGS/EXPENDITURE[2]							
Mortgage/Rent	300.00	300.00	300.00	300.00	300.00	300.00	
Rates/Council Tax[3]	20.84	20.84	20.84	20.84	20.84	20.84	
Services: Water	13.34	13.34	13.34	13.34	13.34	13.34	
Electricity	23.34	23.34	23.34	23.34	23.34	23.34	
Gas	23.34	23.34	23.34	23.34	23.34	23.34	
Stationery & equipment	35.00	35.00	35.00	35.00	35.00	35.00	
Clothing	100.00	100.00	100.00	100.00	100.00	100.00	
Food	300.00	300.00	300.00	300.00	300.00	300.00	
Travel	40.00	40.00	40.00	40.00	40.00	40.00	
General	120.00	120.00	120.00	120.00	120.00	120.00	
	975.86	975.86	975.86	975.86	975.86	975.86	
TOTAL SALES LESS EXPENDITURE	126.64	126.64	126.64	354.64	354.64	354.64	
TOTAL SALES LESS EXPENDITURE CUM[2]	126.64	253.28	379.92	734.56	1,089.20	1,443.84	

Note the difference in the profit lines between Cashflow 1 optimistic forecasting and this pessimistic forecasting.
1. Cum is short for cumulative and it means to keep a running total of the total sales less expenditure line to give a figure representing the amount earned in total (in this case the six month period).
2. Based on fictitious figures.
3. Where bills are not issued monthly, take the annual or quarterly charge and break it down into a monthly charge.

Fig. 14. Example of a pessimistic cashflow forecast.

CASHFLOW 3 – A. N. OTHER – Conservative forecasting – First six months January to June

Based on *seven hour day contract work* and *6 hours in-house typing contract work per week of the period*. Contracting out at *3 months standard secretarial* rate with a slump period in February and March with one week out in the month without work. Slow growth with only three working weeks in the month. No increase in work in first six months.
Rates: Legal – £11.00 per hour; Home contract work – £9.00 per hour; Standard secretarial work – £10.00 per hour.

	Jan	Feb	Mar	Apr	May	June	Total
SALES (FREELANCE CONTRACTS)							
Home typing contracts	180.00	180.00	180.00	180.00	180.00	180.00	
Standard Secretarial contracts (five day week)	1,540.00	1,050.00	1,155.00	1,400.00	1,540.00	1,400.00	
TOTAL CASH RECEIVED	1,720.00	1,230.00	1,335.00	1,580.00	1,720.00	1,580.00	9,165.00
OUTGOINGS/EXPENDITURE[2]							
Mortgage/Rent	300.00	300.00	300.00	300.00	300.00	300.00	
Rates/Council Tax[3]	20.84	20.84	20.84	20.84	20.84	20.84	
Services: Water	13.34	13.34	13.34	13.34	13.34	13.34	
Electricity	23.34	23.34	23.34	23.34	23.34	23.34	
Gas	23.34	23.34	23.34	23.34	23.34	23.34	
Stationery & equipment	35.00	35.00	35.00	35.00	35.00	35.00	
Clothing	100.00	100.00	100.00	100.00	100.00	100.00	
Food	300.00	300.00	300.00	300.00	300.00	300.00	
Travel	40.00	40.00	40.00	40.00	40.00	40.00	
General	120.00	120.00	120.00	120.00	120.00	120.00	
	975.86	975.86	975.86	975.86	975.86	975.86	
TOTAL SALES LESS EXPENDITURE	744.14	254.14	359.14	604.14	744.14	604.14	
TOTAL SALES LESS EXPENDITURE CUM[1]	744.14	998.28	1,357.42	1,961.56	2,075.70	3,309.84	

Note the difference in the profit lines between Cashflow 1 optimistic forecasting, Cashflow 2 pessimistic forecasting and Cashflow 3 conservative forecasting.
1. Cum is short for cumulative and it means to keep a running total of the total sales less expenditure line to give a figure representing the amount earned in total (in this case the six month period).
2. Based on fictitious figures.
3. Where bills are not issued monthly, take the annual or quarterly charge and break it down into a monthly charge.

Fig. 15. Example of a conservative cashflow forecast.

need to consult an accountant. If you wish to incorporate yourself as a limited company you will have to bear further costs and do extra bookwork; moreover, your earnings will be company profits (taxable in 1994 at 25%) and subject to an annual *audit* or accountant's report. Incorporation could cost you £150 to £250.

In accounting terms, it is therefore more time consuming and expensive to be a limited company and you will need to remember that while you may be a director of a limited company, you will be subject to personal taxation under PAYE as a director (assuming of course you draw wages). The company will also be liable to annual corporation tax on any profits remaining after payment of your net wages, PAYE and National Insurance Contributions.

However, there are advantages and these fall in the sphere of *extended* contract work. Many firms and indeed some recruitment agencies will not take on a freelance unless he or she trades as a limited company. The reason is that they do not want to be liable for the national insurance that they might incur if they employed your services on a regular basis. By billing the company or the agency for your hours as a limited company, they will not incur this liability as it is a company that is billing them and not an individual. You should look into this aspect, and if you want to be particularly thorough in your research, you could find out what proportion of firms in your region would or would not take you on without being a limited company. However, if you bill several different clients over the course of a year and you have a Schedule D tax number, you should not have this problem.

Working as a sole trader and limited company at the same time

If you don't want to go into this kind of research, it is possible for you to run the two side by side. For example you could set up your limited company to write your target letters so that you are letting any future client know that they are not looking at a potential national insurance liability. At the same time you can have a simple letterhead which you can bill out on all occasions other than the times when the client insists upon being billed by the limited company. You are covering yourself in all regards by doing this. You will not be precluding yourself from receiving future work and you will be reducing your corporation tax liability. You should also try and find out how your local agencies pay freelances and what sort of bill you would have to submit. However, don't forget the additional costs you will incur in setting up a limited company.

USING ACCOUNTANTS

Selecting an accountant can be difficult. If you are not used to dealing with firms of accountants, you will not know what fees are considered reasonable for your area, or what quality of advice you might be getting. If you choose at random from a telephone book, you are opting for luck of the draw and it could be a costly mistake. One of the most common forms of introduction to a professional firm is by recommendation. If you can consult people you know in business, or talk to those who have had satisfactory dealings with a particular firm of accountants, then it would be advantageous.

The best thing to do is to ring up the Institute of Chartered Accountants (see 'Useful Addresses' at the back of this book). Explain to them the nature and size of your business and discuss your potential requirements with them. They will send you a list, probably a selection of four or five practising firms within your area, who they feel will be suitable for your business and within your price range. You should request an interview with each of them, and you should at the end of these interviews be in a position to choose the firm you feel most comfortable with and believe will offer you a good service.

It is important to ask about their charges per hour, although they will probably want to know what annual turnover you will expect before they can give you an adequate idea of their charges. You really must establish the charges you can reasonably expect per annum and prepare for it in your cashflows. If you have an interview with a firm that is reluctant to discuss fees, go elsewhere. You don't want to end up with the accountant accruing work hours on your behalf and have no idea as to what charge you can expect to pay them.

Questions to ask

At the outset, the sort of questions that you should be asking an accountant are primarily:

- How do I set up an invoice book, invoices paid and received, cash book and petty cash book?

- What sort of expenses can I write off to business?

- What proportion of domestic services, ie electricity, gas, water rates and so on, can I apportion to my business?

- How does PAYE work? Based on my projected earnings, how much should I set aside for tax liability per month?

- Should I register for VAT, what work does it involve and how does it work?

- Are there any particular rules or regulations as far as accounting is concerned in relation to being a freelance?

- What are the advantages and disadvantages of being a limited company, and what effect would this have on my tax liability?

- How much will an annual audit or accountant's report cost me, if I am a limited company? *Note*: the rules governing the auditing of a small company's books are being changed to accommodate small firms and to make the accounting procedure less onerous and expensive. This should be in effect by the end of 1994/1995. When this takes effect, it may render the necessity for an annual audit redundant.

- What happens after I receive a tax assessment?

If you use your premises for your business, some of the costs can be put down as business expenditure. Check with your accountant exactly what you will be able to treat as a business expense.

REGISTERING FOR VALUE ADDED TAX (VAT) PURPOSES

Whether you are required to be registered for VAT or not will depend on your income, or expected income, within the first year. It will involve a lot of bookkeeping and administrative work which, unless you feel it is essential to be registered, is best avoided.

It will of course depend on the Budget each year as to whether your have to register or not. In 1994, for example, you are liable to register for VAT if your expected turnover for the next year will exceed £45,000. You should note that turnover is the amount which you charge your clients; profit is turnover less business expenses.

An accountant will be able to provide you with further information on this and you will see that it is listed above under questions that you should discuss with your accountant. To find out more about VAT without spending money on an accountant, ring up your local HM Customs & Excise office and they will be happy to provide you with a booklet outlining the registration requirements.

The rules for the payment of VAT to HM Customs & Excise are very stringent. The penalties range from fines and, in cases of serious arrears, the possibility of your business being put into liquidation. If your turnover is going to exceed the VAT registration limit, then do be aware before registering that provision will have to be made each quarter for your VAT return form to be completed and the VAT due to be set aside for payment on the due date.

SUMMARY

- Find out if there is an Enterprise Agency operating in your area and if not, where the nearest one is.

- Assess exactly how you wish to start up your business and from this what bookkeeping and accounts information you will need.

- Keep your bookkeeping and administration to a minimum.

- See your bank manager for a preliminary chat – even if you don't want to borrow any money. It never harms to get to know who is running your bank and he or she may have a local branch employee who is specifically paid to look after small businesses. They may have leaflets or information that might be useful.

- Don't be afraid to ask questions.

DISCUSSION POINTS

1. Prepare two pessimistic cashflows using the same method as in figure 15. Use your current income and expenditure for the first cashflow. For the second use the income you are receiving and add on £200 a month for expected earnings from starting up a home typing service. You will need to increase your expenditure to account for the purchase of a computer and stationery.

2. Prepare a conservative cashflow using the same method as in figure 16. Use your current income and an anticipated increase in revenue of £400 from home work. Include your estimated upturn in electricity bills and stationery requirements, and account for the cost of equipment at start-up.

3. Prepare an optimistic cashflow assuming immediate start-up and contract work. Provide two lines for sales figures – one for home work and one for temporary assignments – and create your own estimated earnings, making them optimistic. Use the same expenditure as in preparing your conservative estimate.

7
How to Get Paid and Plan Your Income

INVOICING YOUR CLIENTS

One of the most important aspects of any business is getting your invoices out. It is important, right from the start, that you keep a proper record of work you have carried out. Once the work is completed a bill should be dispatched immediately.

If you are working on a weekly basis for a company, then you should invoice on a weekly basis. Always prepare a timesheet and get it signed on a Friday (or the final day of a weekly contract) to ensure that there could never be a dispute about your hours. Keep a copy for your files and give the original to the client for them to reconcile with your invoice when you submit it.

Once signed, make it a golden rule to translate the hours on your timesheet into an invoice. You will have created your invoice sub-directory in your word processor and set up a proforma invoice for each client. Therefore, your invoices will be to hand with the hourly rate applicable to each client already linked into the invoice document.

Send your invoices off first-class post the day after you have completed a week's contract. If you start to get behind with billing and you leave the bill for anything up to a month, you could be waiting two months for your money if the firm has a policy of paying a month from receipt of invoice (even if you have specified a seven-day payment period).

It is slightly different for in-house work. When you undertake reports or any kind of ongoing work in-house, always bill on completion of the work. This may not necessarily be a week, but two or even three. You simply cannot bill at the end of the week for a job that is only half done. The exceptions to this are very long and difficult jobs which could last anything up to three or four months.

When you take on work such as this, you should agree at the beginning of the contract an interim billing date. Give the client an estimate of the length of time the work is likely to take you, and the dates on which you intend to submit an interim bill and a final billing date. Remember, the client has to do cashflows too and will want to know his or her likely costs.

Try to work out at the beginning what type of work you are going to bill either weekly or on an interim basis. On the whole you should aim to bill on a weekly basis for weekly contracts. Invoice undefined small in-house jobs on completion. For lengthy and difficult work agree an interim and end billing date. When billing, a golden rule to remember is always type on the bottom of your invoice PAYMENT WITHIN SEVEN DAYS. This will cover you as far as terms and conditions are concerned, and if you ever experience non-payment of an invoice, the clear message of seven days to pay will be taken as evidence of your terms and acceptance of them by the company you billed.

GETTING PAID AND PAYING POLICIES

Assert yourself firmly, but courteously, about being paid. It really is essential to get this right from the outset. People on the whole will expect you to ask. If you submit a bill at the end of each week of a contract, you have every right to know when you are going to be paid for it.

Try not to make enemies in the accounts department if you can possibly help it! If you submit a bill you should already know by this stage when it is going to be settled. Things do go wrong sometimes. Computers fail, or invoices do occasionally get lost and any number of other things can happen. If you are not receiving payments for work done, you will need to either ring up, or go and see if you are working in the firm, what has happened to your money. People won't mind you asking but don't let yourself get annoyed about it.

You are in a better position than most when freelancing within a firm to just pop into the accounts department and collect your cheque. If you deal with matters correctly most of the time your invoices will receive fairly prompt attention.

When it comes to payment of a bill, many firms (particularly larger ones) have paying policies for invoices, weekly, monthly – sometimes quarterly. When you first meet a new client, find out what their paying policy is. If you don't, you will not know how to forecast your own income. You may experience frustrating delays and wonder why. On the whole, firms tend to be fairly flexible with freelance secretaries and, except in rare circumstances, you should always be paid fairly promptly.

However, if you do run across problems, such as late payment, there are a number of avenues that you can pursue, but before doing so ask yourself whether you want to work for that company again. If they provide you with regular work, you are going to have to weigh up how slow the payment is against possible future income. It is very unwise ever to use threatening behaviour unless there is no other way. This is very difficult and can require great patience, but there could be a genuine misunderstanding. If you become aggressive the relationship will undoubtedly be permanently severed.

It may be wisest to let it go the first time, and if it happens again or continuously, weigh up the 'hassle' factor it is causing you against the amount of work you are actually receiving. If the proportion doesn't warrant the amount of time you are having to spend chasing up payment, it may be best to 'call it a day' and cut your losses.

If all else fails and you have already severed the relationship a solicitor's letter is a method of recovering payment. However, freelances are usually amongst those who get paid fairly promptly. For professional information on recovery of debt, your local Enterprise Agency, Citizens Advice Bureau or local solicitor will be able to advise you more fully.

Firms in financial trouble

Watch out for companies in liquidation or receivership. It is unlikely that you will come across this, because once this stage has been reached, it is doubtful if your services would be contracted in the first place. Be aware, however, that if you are working for a company just before it is about to go into receivership and your bill has not been settled, it is extremely unlikely that you will ever be paid; any effort to regain your money once it is in receivership is really throwing good money after bad. You will not be among what is termed the **secured list of creditors**. Secured creditors may include banks, solicitors, accountants, staff, and so on; the **unsecured creditors** are usually those who trade with the firm, ie service companies, contractors and sub-contractors. You will come under the heading of service and you will stand little or no chance of being paid. If you detect signs of a company becoming 'unhealthy', cut your losses quickly!

WHEN TO RAISE YOUR RATES

Your should have aimed for balance in your pricing structure. You will invariably have different charge out rates for different types of firms and for different types of work. While there is scope for adapting your prices to different markets, the scope for big increases is not very great. During your first year you will learn much by trial and error, and a lot of time will be devoted to building up your confidence and establishing relationships with people. After the first year of being freelance you will be familiar with the possibilities and opportunities that exist within the sector/sectors that you service.

You should have apportioned in percentages the type of work you are receiving, ie the amount of in-house work, the amount of contracting out work and the amount of 'one-off' jobs you have received. If you are thinking of raising your hourly rate you will need to take the following into account:

- general economic conditions

- the financial condition of the firm for whom you want to raise your rate

- your relationship with the client

- your usefulness to the company

- the type of work you are undertaking

- any training you have undertaken to keep in 'step' with the firm's word processing requirements

- the area you live and work in.

Don't just raise the hourly rate by percentage on a yearly basis. You may lose work if the client decides that you are becoming too expensive. Not only that, but it will cause offence if you don't discuss it first. Be aware also of pricing yourself out of the market.

When economic conditions are favourable, you should be able to renegotiate your hourly rates. If you have established good relationships with clients over a period of time, you will find in years to come much value in those good relationships. You will be able to charge slightly more. If a firm you do regular work for is going through difficult times, stick with them on a lower rate. They will appreciate it and you will have work. When things do improve, they will be sympathetic to giving you an increase.

FIXING FREELANCE INCOME

We have discussed 'fixing' contracts that are going to come up every year and thereby enable you to build on contracts that you established in year one, to carry on in to year two.

There are two separate approaches to 'fixing' freelance work.

- Building up separate day of the week contracts that take place regularly and thereby fixing and anchoring your income and your circle of contacts.

- Taking incidental in-house work and building on this and contracting out on a weekly basis as and when work arises.

The ideal situation would be to have a different firm to see on each of the five working days of the week, but the reality of achieving this is extremely difficult. If it were possible at first attempt, you would have guaranteed income and a handful of contacts that you service every day each year. Your annual income would be guaranteed and the amount of effort needed for marketing kept to a minimum. But this is not something to bank on. Consider the time factor involved. It takes a long time for the right opportunities to come up that fit in with each other.

It could take a year or more before you receive one enquiry which may be an offer for two days' work a week. However, while the offer may look attractive at first glance, it is of little use to you on its own. It would have been better if at the same time as you were offered two days a week from another firm, and even better if a third firm offered you one day – thereby filling up five working days with contracts that are fixed. But say you do not get such offers. Say you only have the enquiry from one firm for two days of the week? What will you do for the other three days? If you accept the offer from the firm for say, a Tuesday and a Thursday every week, what will you then do if any of the other companies you have approached ring you up with an offer for a two-week booking? You won't be able to take it. You could end up turning away a high proportion of work and thereby losing money by accepting the two days' work.

If you can afford (or want only part time work) to take it on while you wait for another offer from another firm, then all well and good. If you are a mother and want to earn extra cash, this would be quite a suitable arrangement and you may want to start up your business slowly like this. You will be able to fit your working hours around taking the children to and picking them up from school, and perhaps take some in-house work as well. But if you need regular weekly contracts for a large percentage of the year, by accepting the two days a week you are tying yourself down to an undesirable contract. It is not a good idea even to consider this during the first year. Better to have a week without work and take the risks, or go to a recruitment agency on a temporary basis, than to give the impression of being unavailable to potentially new clients.

Implications of fixed contracts

Fixing your income can have many different implications. You should start to think of income not just in terms of work secured, but hours spent in arranging meetings, working for different clients and expansion of your contacts.

However, if you are offered a two day a week contract, don't turn it down outright. Use your negotiating skills to see what sort of work it is and how it needs to be carried out each week. For example, is it of an immediate nature, that is, do you need to be on the premises between normal office hours? Is it a large or a small firm you are dealing with? Can the work be rearranged to suit you? A small firm may not need a secretary whose presence is required in the office, but simply a certain amount of typing two days a week. If the latter is the case, you could have a fixed contract if you want it by using your powers of persuasion to turn it into an evening and/or weekend job. If you do that you are receiving the money for a fixed contract, but you are not tying up your available daily hours for any other incidental work or temporary assignments that you may be offered.

When people get to know you and your reliability, they will adapt to different ways of working with you. The market is not very big for in-house typing work. Such agencies that specialise in it are usually located in large office complexes or in the heart of cities and towns and usually operate the service as a sideline to recruiting activities, thus minimising their risks.

The second approach to freelance work is not to work on the assumption of receiving in-house work, but merely work out your potential for contracting out. In this event, you may not need to buy machinery and equipment – suffice to lease equipment to do your approach letters and résumé and await responses. This will minimise your overheads, but does limit your potential locally.

By doing this you will be relying on weekly work that comes in through the year. However, while reducing your capital outlay, it does limit your adaptability, and adaptability is the key to success in any business. It will also reduce your earning capacity.

That said, if you can work on the assumption that you will aim to build up a regular amount of fixed work with companies during certain times of the year, you should be able to make enough to carry you through the slack periods.

This again relates back to the target areas that you choose. The amount of preparatory work that you do is much like laying the foundations of a house. If it is done properly and thoroughly, and in the case of target areas broadly enough, you should be able to establish such contracts. If you limit your scope, or if the region you approach is too narrow, you will not get enough response to build upon.

GOING WHERE THE MONEY IS

You can save yourself a lot of time and effort by following economic trends. Do not approach companies at an economically bad time. If a particular trade or industry is going through a slump, you can still approach them with a view to the future, but your expectation should be for the future and not for the present. Research the successful companies in your area or region, to see which are most likely to secure you an immediate income and which are best to keep in mind longer term.

If you are a freelance secretary with in-depth knowledge of a particular field which has been affected by a recession, it would be foolhardy to direct all your efforts onto such a field and expect successful results. Be aware of economic trends, and cast your net in several directions to achieve an essential balance.

It could be that a recession will work in your favour as a freelance secretary. During any economic downturn redundancies will take place. Rather than taking the risks of employing someone full time, you could find that companies who have made staff redundancies will want to contract out work on an 'as and when' basis and you could be in demand.

Also, there may be a slump in a market in one region of the UK, but prosperity and growth in that same market elsewhere. By following what is happening in your region you are making yourself aware of the possibilities that are open to you either currently or for the future.

By researching the economic situation in your region you will be able to obtain information on the companies and professions that are trading, what their annual turnover is, the type of work that they do, the number of employees in the firm and what types of firms are doing well. In other words, weigh up information in the light of economic conditions. From looking at the number of employees, you will be able to assess roughly the size of the company and the likely number of support staff within the firm. Do not, however, as mentioned earlier, be put off by the apparent size of a company. If it is listed as having six employees, don't by-pass it for the purpose of your mailshot because you anticipate that a company of such a small size will not be able to provide you with work; the reverse may be the case.

Learning from responses to your mailshots

A useful exercise is to make comparisons after you have chosen groups of firms that you wish to target. Estimate how many responses you are likely to receive and how many of them will be for what type of work. When you do get responses compare the number of responses with what you anticipated. If the number you receive is near to your guess, then when undertaking future mailshots, work along the same expectations. If not, review your method of assessing likely responses. It is better to be slightly pessimistic and then you can only be pleasantly surprised. Whatever you do, don't send out 150 letters and expect to get 150 relies back. If you get 10 to 20 replies you will be doing well.

By doing this, you will be able to concentrate on where the opportunities lie. For example, if you are receiving a high percentage response from one sector and a poor one from another, try to analyse the likely reasons and maybe modify your next approach to accommodate likely factors.

After a year of 'testing the water' in this way, you may want to begin writing to a further group or group of companies and you will have the experience to base your approach on tried and tested methods.

Adapting to the technology

If you are skilled on several word processing systems, you will find that you can adapt your skills to almost any environment. If you are

familiar with a word processing package, for example, which you
have always used in one particular environment and so know well
only some of its functions, look into the capabilities of the package
to see how you can apply them to other fields. You will be
upgrading your knowledge at the same time as widening the fields
that you can approach. Perhaps you have a word processing system
with a high graphics compatibility, but does your PC have the right
capability and memory to run graphics? Knowing your word
processing packages thoroughly will help you in determining exactly
what kind of work you can do for other people and what you will
have to turn away.

WHAT SORT OF INCOME CAN I EXPECT?

There is no cut and dried answer to this as it depends on several
factors:

- the location you are in

- your price structuring

- how hard you are prepared to work

- what sort of contracts you aim for and what type of work you
  are going to undertake

- what skills you are offering.

The location you are in
If you have done your research at the outset, you will know what
sort of rates per hour you can charge in the region in which you live
and aim to work. In London, for example, the rates are higher than
in the regions, because of the high costs of living in the capital. You
cannot simply adopt a pricing structure that works in one region
and apply it to another.

Your price structuring
The location you are in is not the only determining factor in your
price structuring. There is a fundamental key in price structuring
which should also be observed.
    If you have made a study of the sort of fees that an agency in your

region would charge, it is not the case that you need drastically to undercut the agency. You may like to start your initial prospect letter by charging say only 50p or £1.00 less per hour.

If you offer your services too cheaply, it can have the same effect as selling above the odds. If you ask a very low price per hour, companies may think you are no good, and so not use your services. In the main, most firms want good service for the price they are paying and if your service is good they will pay the market rate for it. On the other hand, they may try you out and laugh all the way to the bank when they realise what an excellent service they are getting on the cheap! There's no need to let yourself be exploited. Remember, reliability and security play a large part in persuading a firm to use your services rather than going through a recruitment agent. If you are good at what you do, you won't have to sell yourself short to obtain a contract.

How hard and what hours you are prepared to work

This can only be determined by you. Only you know what your available working hours are and what you are prepared to invest in effort. As with most things, what you put in is by and large what you get out. You will have an advantage above many small businesses – all the administration will be free – you will be doing it yourself, and being a secretary you will probably be very good at it. This good organisation will leave you free to put everything into the business, if you want to.

If you want high financial rewards, there is no question that you will have to work hard, but they are there. It is up to you.

What sort of contracts you aim for

As a general rule, the more specialist work that you undertake, the more money you will be able to command. Examples of specialist work are:

- long arbitration documentation – international arbitrations

- translation typing

- tape interviews

- taped conference transcriptions

- technical books/manuals

- presentation work – desk top publishing.

When you start out the market may not be big enough for specialist work alone and you will have to compromise. Also, you will not be well enough known to 'pick and choose'. But you can aim in this direction while undertaking other contracts to earn a base income.

It may be that you will receive a proportion of specialised work and it may be that you will be called upon again the following year. Gradually, you will build a reputation for being able to do this kind of work.

What skills you are offering
The more you are prepared to widen your skills and become very good at technical work, then, of course, the more you can charge.

CASE STUDIES

Juanita Malette
Juanita has completed a year of freelancing. She has not done badly. She had a few weeks out of work in January but she has managed. It is now August and she is returning to Hope Hassle, a large firm of solicitors, to undertake a summer assignment. Juanita is on a good rate with the firm and she occasionally uses her Spanish skills in the shipping department of the firm for translation work.

Things haven't been easy over the last year as the recession has hit not only the housing market but industry and the professions. However, Juanita considers that it is reasonable to raise her rates by 10% to this particular client. 'They're a big firm and they can afford it,' she thinks ' and, besides, I do all that translation work at my ordinary rates.' She looks through her word processing directory for invoices and pulls up the Hope Hassle invoice proforma. She changes the £10.80 per hour to an increased 10%, rounding the figure of £11.88 up to £11.90 per hour.

After the first week, she submits a timesheet and the invoice to John Endleby, the personnel manager with whom she normally deals.

The following Monday while she is working at her desk, she receives a telephone call from John. 'Hello Juanita, could you come round and see me when you have a minute.' Juanita agrees and goes to his office at lunchtime.

'Ah, Juanita. Sit down. I had a look at your invoice on Friday night and I see that you have increased the rate per hour – why was that?'

Juanita feels uncomfortable. 'Well, I just thought because of the translation work and having worked here for a year, it was appropriate to increase the rate by 10%.'

'Well, I'm sorry to hear that, Juanita, because the firm simply can't afford it – times are very difficult and I would have appreciated a discussion with you first about it. I'm afraid, that unless you can lower it, we won't be able to continue using you, which will be a pity.'

Juanita has handled things badly. She should have discussed the matter first and not been left in a position of sitting red faced in front of the personnel manager feeling very embarrassed, and also forced into a position of either backing down or losing the contract.

Jenny Anglesea

Jenny has established a wide network of solicitors that she works for and is currently on contract to a firm for the next two weeks. About a month ago she did a mailshot to a market that she was not totally familiar with but felt she would be able to cope with – the hotel and catering trade. She has received an interested response and has an appointment to see John Kerouac of Felte Group Catering.

Up until now her contracts for temping have been fairly straightforward in that she receives weekly payments for her work.

She negotiates a booking with Felte Group Catering after meeting Mr Kerouac to commence in two weeks' time for two months. They agree rates per hour and Jenny is looking forward to working in the new offices and in a new field in which she hasn't worked before.

At the end of the first week she prepares a timesheet and takes it to Mr Kerouac's office. 'I wonder if you'd mind signing my timesheet and I'll bring my invoice in on Monday if that's all right with you?'

'That's fine Jenny and thank you for your hard work this week.'

Jenny goes home pleased and has enjoyed her week in a new environment. The following week she takes her invoice in and hands it to Mr Kerouac. When she hasn't received payment by Friday and it is time to take in her next timesheet for signature, she tentatively brings up the subject of payment.

'Oh, didn't I tell you? Head office in Scotland does all the bills quarterly.' Seeing Jenny's aghast face Mr Kerouac said kindly, 'I'll speak to them and see if we can make an exception – I thought you had realised. How do you get paid normally?'

'Well, weekly as a rule – I haven't prepared at all for being paid quarterly. If you could do something I'd be extremely grateful.'

Jenny should have asked at the interview about paying policies. If something cannot be arranged for payment of her bills monthly, it is going to be three months before she receives payment for her first bill, leaving her very much out of pocket and having to negotiate a short notice overdraft facility with her bank.

Suzi Jenson

Suzi has also branched out. She recently got an enquiry by recommendation from an accountant's client who writes books.

Jacki Baggins has been working on compiling a book from taped interviews about people who've undergone traumatic experiences in their lives. She gives Suzi a call.

'I'm writing a book and have over 26 interviews on tape already – the only thing is that some of the interviews are a bit muffled and distressing – would that bother you? Only I'm having a bit of trouble finding somebody who could do the job.'

Suzi thinks quickly. This, in her view, is specialist work and she had every right to charge a higher rate – at the same time she'd have to be frank and tell Jacki that she was out on contract during the day and would only be able to produce the work at evenings and weekends.

'Yes, I'd like to do the work for you but I do have to tell you that I charge slightly more for work of this nature, and I am out on contract during the day. My standard rate is £13.50 per hour and for long jobs such as this I usually agree an interim billing date. Of course, I'd have to listen to a tape first and transcribe some work for you and if you are happy with the work and the rates, we would take it from there.'

'You don't charge by the tape then or by the page?'

'Well, no. If I did that, and it is a particularly difficult section, it would take me maybe a lot longer than, say, another tape and I would be losing out.'

'OK, well that sounds reasonable. Could you come round and see me and have a listen to the tapes and we'll agree rates and payment dates at that time?'

Suzi has dealt with the situation well. She capitalises straight away on the situation realising that there is more money in this type of work than in her standard contracts and is also honest with the new client about her availability. She also immediately realises that the work may take her some time and mentions billing on an interim basis.

SUMMARY

- Always produce your invoices promptly on completion of work.

- Always find out about paying policies and how they relate to your being paid.

- Always take economic conditions into consideration before raising rates.

- Consider the amount of work you get from a firm before raising your rates.

- Always discuss a proposed rate with the client first.

Never:

- Just raise your rates without discussion.

- Assume that payment will be weekly.

- Aim too high and price yourself out of the market.

DISCUSSION POINTS

1. You have acquired a new skill which you are applying with a firm for which you have worked for over a year. You feel that it is appropriate for you to raise your rates. The firm gives you a lot of work and are making redundancies. What do you do?

2. You are at an interview for work in an area of commerce you have not undertaken before. You ask the interviewer about

paying policies and she tells you that bills are only settled quarterly. The offer of work is for two months. You have other contacts on a lesser rate who have also asked for your services. What points do you have in mind before saying yes or no to the new contract?

3. You have just been offered a long arbitration which has been recorded on tape for transcription. It's very difficult work. What terms do you think would be appropriate for (a) scheduling of this work (b) being paid? How do you discuss this with the client?

How to Write a Report
John Bowden

Written by an experienced manager and staff trainer, this well-presented handbook provides a very clear step-by-step framework for every individual, whether dealing with professional colleagues, customers, clients, suppliers or junior or senior staff. Contents: Preparation and planning. Collecting and handling information. Writing the report. Improving your thinking. Improving presentation. Achieving a good writing style. Making effective use of English. Illustrations. Choosing paper, covers and binding. Appendices, glossary, index. John Bowden BSc(Econ) MSc has long experience both as a professional manager in industry, and as a Senior Lecturer running courses in accountancy, auditing, and effective communication, up to senior management level.

£7.99, 160pp illus. 1 85703 035 4.

Please add postage & packing (UK £1.00 per copy. Europe £2.00 per copy. World £3.00 per copy airmail).

How To Books Ltd, Plymbridge House, Estover Road, Plymouth PL6 7PZ, United Kingdom. Tel: (0752) 695745. Fax: (0752) 695699. Telex: 45635.

Credit card orders may be faxed or phoned.

8
Diplomacy, Negotiation and Communication Skills

BEING ALL THINGS TO ALL PEOPLE

Negotiating skills are an obvious necessity. Running a freelance secretarial business is different from, for example, being a manufacturer. You are not providing a product which people may buy anyway: you are selling yourself and have to sell yourself through negotiation. Without good communication skills and a certain degree of diplomacy you could find yourself in difficulties.

Having established your company or your freelance services, there are certain abilities you need to be successful at it, that is, the ability to:

- work with anyone in any environment

- be all things to all people

- negotiate prices and terms at management level on the one hand and, on the other, work well and get on with the people you are placed with

- negotiate with the accounts department to get your invoices settled.

You will not be judged by the personnel department on the standard of your work alone. You will also be judged on your ability to mix and communicate with other people.

If you have difficulty in working with others you may not find yourself back with that particular company again. You must get on with your colleagues but keep in mind that you have a business to run: services for payment, straight and simple. To get too involved (or, to be too remote) is not a good situation to be in.

Being discreet about your earnings

Once you have negotiated fees for your work with a company –
whether it be long or short term – it is the 'kiss of death' to discuss
this with anybody other than the person who contracted your
services. If you don't observe this rule, it could very easily lead to
difficulties. There could be other temporaries from agencies who are
doing work at the same time as you who are not getting the same
money from the agency as you are by contracting direct. It could
lead to jealousy, loss of motivation by other staff and dislike of you.
It will certainly not please the personnel department if rumours are
circulating back to them that you have been talking about your
earnings, so tact and diplomacy are of vital importance.

You, almost certainly, will be asked! People are interested in money
and how to get it. If you are freelancing in any company, the first
question that other secretaries or other temporary secretaries will ask
you is what agency you are from. As you are not from an agency you
will have to say that you approached the company directly. This in turn
will lead to all number of questions, because it will be of interest to
others who would like to consider doing what you have done.

You should try to stick to the truth as much as possible but never
say how much you earn on an hourly basis. One way of avoiding it is
by simply showing your reluctance to discuss it.

Remaining businesslike

The level of involvement you want in discussions such as these, or in
the office generally, ought to be minimal. That does not preclude
you from making friends or acquaintances, but if you get too
involved or give away too much information it could start to cause
problems. Primarily, you are running a business and everything you
do while on a client's premises is preparatory work for your future.
You are your own agent and marketing yourself; if you become too
involved in 'company politics' you will be treading a dangerous
path, perhaps finding yourself involved in petty squabbles and
difficult staff relations. They are best avoided. Of course it is not
always easy to tolerate a particularly tedious situation – it's just a
question of learning when to 'avoid the slings' and in which way to
'throw the arrows back'.

The more of an 'all rounder' you can be, and the more you can be
all things to all people, the more success you are likely to have.
There are going to be companies where you will find it difficult to
work with certain people, because there are people who are just

extremely difficult. But the more you are prepared for this the better equipped you will be to deal with it.

Nearly all secretarial work is about being a good communicator, and providing a good service. The demands are usually immediate and you are being called upon because there is an overload or a shortage of staff. Service is what it's all about and it's an important word to remember. If there are difficult situations, you should weigh up how tolerable or intolerable they are before reacting. If you end up working for someone difficult, try to grin and bear it. Say nothing. If you get a reputation with the personnel department for being able to work with all types and manner of people, and more particularly with people who are known to be difficult, you are going to be asked for without question time after time. It may be hard, but it's good business sense and it really does get easier.

Unlike a shop, people do not just wander in off the street because they had a need for an item and a quick purchase ensues. When you sell yourself as a freelance secretary, you are constantly on the shelf being examined; you are never taken to the cash register! You need to relate to people not only for the present but for the future as well. You are not just walking into an office to see the personnel manager about the service you can provide and that is the end of it. That is the easy part, the beginning.

The first time you undertake an assignment with a client you will show your skills and performance and a report will go back to personnel on your ability. However relaxed a situation may seem, remember that you are being assessed either directly or indirectly.

Try to be placid without being a pushover. Be courteous, without overdoing it. However much you may want to talk about your achievements, it really does pay dividends to listen to other people.

It may be difficult, because, having set up your own company and learned how to run your own business successfully, when you are on the client's premises, you will have to reverse your role. You are then the accommodator. However much you feel that things could be managed better or done in a different way, it is better to hold back the advice and simply do what you are being paid to do.

MANAGING DIFFICULT PEOPLE AND DIFFICULT SITUATIONS

When to assert yourself

There will still be times when you have to assert yourself. It is unavoidable. There may be a situation where you are working with a person who just simply doesn't like you and is really making life very difficult indeed. Never lose your temper – it is unbelievably damaging. Assert yourself by being firm and if it is really an impossible situation, walk away from it. It is better to leave without an argument than to sever ties with the firm by getting entangled in rows.

Offices are full of people of different backgrounds, temperaments and professionalism – all of whom have different functions within the firm. Some people are impatient, demanding – others easy-going and pleasant. As a freelance secretary you are called upon to work with all manner of people and it is not always plain sailing.

It is best to deal with rudeness by being firm but polite; with impatience by calmness; with anger by refusal to be angry back. It is not always easy to remember this in the heat of the moment, but if you can bear it in mind it will help.

In pressurised environments, tempers can fly. Try to see it for what it is: a bad day in the office, or a particularly difficult working environment. Do consider the length of your contract. If it is only for a week, then you will soon be able to walk away from it. If the contract is for a three-month booking and you feel that you would not be able to manage in the particular environment under such conditions, then cut your losses. You won't be in positions such as these very often, but it happens.

The best thing to do is not just 'up sticks', but to bear it for a week and then go to see the person who contracted you. Explain that you feel you just can't work in that department and state your reasons. It may mean moving you to another department or the end of work with that firm, so weigh up the considerations carefully. If it is a smaller office and you don't feel comfortable, you will have to say so and look to other firms or contacts for work.

If something feels wrong for you, then go with your feelings; don't just stick at it and make yourself miserable. If it's not working, move on. If you have targeted enough firms and established good relations with enough people, you won't be out of work for long.

USING THE CLIENT'S EQUIPMENT

When you agree to work in a company you should ask about calling your answering machine a certain number of times each day. You should not find this a problem as your client will realise that you need to keep in touch with other clients. Do check first though – it is only courteous. I make a point of limiting my calls to returning those that are on my answering machine. Any personal calls I make outside office hours, unless absolutely unavoidable.

In large corporations and companies, telephones are often monitored for calls because of losses incurred through over-use by staff. Many firms have call-barring devices attached to staff telephones to reduce the risk of such expenditure. Some firms allow a certain proportion of private calls and anything over the limit is charged to the member of staff by way of a weekly bill.

Do, therefore, check if the extension you are using has a monitor on it for outgoing calls. If the call monitoring system has been applied and you are replacing a secretary who is on holiday, she will be less than amused if she comes back to a bill for your telephone calls. British Telecom have a Chargecall card which charges back to your own number. Enquire into this and, if you feel it necessary, get one so that in the event of working for a very strict company you will not be made to feel uncomfortable about having to use the telephone.

It would be unprofessional to use a client's equipment for any work of your own. It may seen a trifling point, but you should aim not to type personal correspondence using anything but your own machinery.

CASE STUDIES

Juanita Malette

Alistair Heep is a local surveyor. He has already shouted at the recruitment agency he normally deals with for not providing him with a temp immediately he needed one.

'That blasted girl has gone off sick for the week again and there's typing to be done – why haven't you got anyone? Oh never mind.' He slams the phone down. He turns to his wife, 'Where's that Malette girl's details, have you got them still – I suppose we'll have to give her a ring'.

His wife rummages about in an old filing cabinet and pulls out some papers. 'Here they are – she's expensive though!'

Mr Heep grabs the paper huffing and puffing and dials Juanita's number.

Juanita has had a week at home. She is between contracts. She receives the call from Mr Heep.

'He doesn't sound very nice, but it's a good rate – I might as well go along – it's only up the road.'

On getting to the office she finds it is small and chaotic and that Mr Heep often has the administration staff in tears.

It isn't long before he comes in and starts picking on Juanita. 'Your prices are very high for a typist, don't you think? Normally I go to a recruitment agency but the blasted people couldn't get me anyone today otherwise I wouldn't have had to pay these sorts of rates.' Juanita works through the morning, seething. In the afternoon Mr Heep brings all her typing back and throws it on the desk. 'You really think that's worth what you're charging?'

'That's it! I've had it with you – find yourself another poor wretch – as far as I'm concerned you can stick it you loathsome man!' With that, Juanita picks up her things, shoves the signature book off the side of the table and storms out.

While this is a pretty horrendous situation, Juanita should have handled it differently. She shouldn't have let Mr Heep get to her. When he attacked her about her rates, she should have asked him calmly whether he would like her to leave. She would have turned the decision back to him. He needed her, but by letting him get to her by becoming angry she has lost out. The contract was just for the week and it would have been better not to react.

Jenny Anglesea
One of the secretaries in the office where Jenny is currently working is very inquisitive about what Jenny is earning. Tracey Double has been with the firm 15 years and is a great talker – about everyone in the office and everything that goes on there. 'How did you come to be working for us then? What agency are you from?'

'I'm not from an agency actually – I approached the firm directly.'

'That's a good idea. What made you do that?'

'Well I wanted to try and see if I could be a freelance for a while.' Jenny thought, 'She's just going to keep on asking me questions, I know she is.'

'How long have you been doing it then?'

'Oh, about a year – something like that.'

'That's good, you must be doing OK then?'

'Not too badly, but you know with the recession and everything it's been difficult at times.' 'I must play it down,' thinks Jenny, 'otherwise she'll never leave me alone.'

'My sister's thinking about doing something like that – what sort of money do you think she could earn?'

'Well, it depends really.'

'On what?'

'Well, where she lives, what sort of skills she's got, that kind of thing.'

'What do you get per hour then?'

Jenny goes red with embarrassment. 'Well I can't really say, it's difficult.'

Tracey goes off eventually and at lunchtime she says to her friend, 'That temp must be earning at fortune – do you know she wouldn't tell me what her hourly rate was, just looked embarrassed. It's not fair, getting all that money!'

Jenny was right not to say what her hourly rate was, but she should have been more assertive with Tracey. She was on the defensive throughout the conversation. When Tracey mentioned her sister, she should have said something like 'What an excellent idea, I'll have a chat with her sometime but I really have to get on at the moment – sorry.' She should have been assertive but friendly.

Suzi Jenson

The word processing department in a large firm that Suzi has worked for on several occasions have got three people on maternity leave. Janice in personnel gives Suzi a ring eight weeks before Christmas to see if she is interested in a long-term booking in the department.

Suzi takes the assignment. She knows that the word processing supervisor has an awful reputation for being a subtle bully. She winds the girls up and generally makes their daily lives pretty miserable.

Suzi thinks about her holiday over Christmas and thinks about the future with the firm. She knows that there will be a lot of future work and she has had a good income from them. She considers that for eight weeks the situation is manageable.

When she gets there it is every bit as bad as she has anticipated but she is determined to see it through until Christmas.

The word processing supervisor gives her all the long and difficult jobs to do, but Suzi sees this as a blessing. She looks at it positively. The busier she is, the more anaesthetised she will be during her working day until Christmas and the more she will be able to switch off.

Some days it does make her miserable and depressed, but every time she feels bad, she thinks about her holiday and the fact that it is not a permanent situation. She carries on. She avoids confrontation and successfully finishes the contract.

At the end of the period she goes to see Janice in personnel and states her case. 'I love the firm and I like coming here a lot but if it is at all possible, I would prefer not to work in the word processing department again.'

Janice gives Suzi a knowing nod. 'Yes, I understand – she is known about in the firm. I can see that it has been difficult for you. Thanks for doing it anyway.'

Suzi has done the right thing. She has taken the overall picture and put the situation into perspective. She has decided it is tolerable for a certain period, but politely and firmly she has stated that she wouldn't really be happy working in those circumstances again. The fact that she has stuck it out in the first place puts her in a strong position and very tactfully she has managed to extricate herself from having to go into the department again in the future, without severing links with the firm.

SUMMARY

- Be pleasant but firm.

- Be assertive without being aggressive.

- Never 'tell' people, 'ask' them, eg 'I need my bill paying today!' should be phrased as 'Do you think it would be possible to pay my bill within the next week?'

- Don't be afraid to negotiate with people.

- Remember, when you are on the client's premises you are the accommodator.

- Take an interest in people.

DISCUSSION POINTS

1. Using the case studies above as a guideline, prepare three fictitious situations which could pose you with problems at work and write out your way of dealing with them.

2. You have had ten or eleven messages left on your answering machine and they are all calls which you have to return while at work. You envisage that some of them could take some time. The firm you are working for don't mind you using the phone. Do you go ahead and make all the calls? If not, what do you think you should do?

3. Somebody has shared a confidence with you about another girl in the office being an alcoholic. Apparently she keeps a bottle of vodka in the drawer of the desk where you are going to be sitting. You are worried about this in case someone thinks it is yours. What do you do?

9
What About the Future?

'Large streams from little fountains flow,
Tall oaks from little acorns grow.'

David Everett

UPGRADING YOUR SKILLS

Do aim to upgrade your skills whenever possible. Keep your eyes
and ears open for developments in word processing software, where
they originate from and to what market they are geared.

As mentioned in chapter 2, there has been a widespread
movement away from dedicated word processing systems to
desktop multi-purpose workstations, as the requirements for the
PC to be available not only to secretaries but to all levels of
management and administrators has exploded. Secretaries' levels of
experience need to be broader than ever before. They are no longer
simply required to be word processor operators but are expected to
adapt to working in a PC environment. This means using

- networked systems

- desktop publishing packages

- mail sending packages such as **E'Mail**

- **fax box** operation within a PC

- spreadsheet and graphics software, and

- databases.

While firms provide training courses for the staff they expect to perform on these PCs, there still seems to be a basic unawareness of how much knowledge it actually takes to operate software to its full advantage.

This is particularly true in the case of secretaries. Many secretaries are sent on basic courses for operation of new software in a management attempt to save money. Had they invested money in more detailed training at the outset, they would be upgrading the skills of their support staff to perform many multi-purpose tasks on PCs, so obviating the need for management or lower management to waste time on tasks that their PA/secretary could perfectly well do for them. The position is improving, but slowly. Many secretaries say that, had they had more than basic training, they would have saved valuable time while word processing by knowing more than the basic commands to operate their system/word processing package.

It is vitally important to keep abreast of technology. Subscribe to institutes and magazines which keep you informed of changes and the effect of these changes to the field(s) you work in. Allow yourself a fair-sized budget for this. It will reward you in the long run.

Training courses and certificates

As you become aware of new software or systems, enrol on training courses to upgrade your skills. If you are doing this while on contract with a firm that is changing over its system, tell the person who hired you; tell them that because you are not knowledgeable on the new system they are adopting, you are funding yourself through a training course. When you have completed it, give them a copy of your certificate (certificates are normally issued by most of the training firms, when a course has been completed successfully by a candidate) for their file. It shows initiative on your part and it will keep you in work with that particular firm.

Secretarial colleges run courses in shorthand, typing and many word processing programs for further upgrading your skills, or to adopt a new skill. Independent companies run software and hardware courses geared to accommodate the varying levels of experience – look in your local paper and *Yellow Pages* for advertisements. Specialist press will also run advertisements, and you may receive information on courses with institute mailings.

If you do further training, find out what you can from your trainer about what sort of firms are buying this kind of software, eg is it being snapped up by the legal profession, the banking profession, insurance markets, and so on? This established, check your mailshot lists to see if you have approached firms who might be changing to this software. If you have, write to them again with a copy of your certificate. You will be able to state that you have now upgraded your skills and that you are attaching a copy of your certificate of competence. It is professional and its shows dedication.

Training courses are not cheap. But if it is going to open doors for you and increase your earning power, it is money well spent.

The overall purpose of training is to keep abreast of current changes. If you do not keep pace with developments in word processing packages available and the ones coming on to the market, and the changes in working patterns, you are in danger of cutting yourself off from future sources of work. The whole essence of training is preparing for the future. It is so easy to live in the present thinking about immediate skills and the immediate workload. By dedicating a proportion of your time to future needs and future office requirements, you will keep ahead of the competition and ensure a future for yourself.

When thinking about training, take into consideration other skills or qualifications that you may find useful to broaden your horizons. If you decide to expand and take on assistance, you will need more business skills, marketing ideas and staff management skills.

SUB-CONTRACTING

If you are receiving more work than you can handle, you may want to consider sub-contracting. However, before you get to this stage, you should have individuals in mind whom you feel produce quality work and on whom you can rely. Sub-contracting to other freelances is fine, so long as you are sure of the skills and capabilities of the person you wish to sub-contract to.

Remember that a recruitment agency is only as good as the staff that it employs. In the same way, if you sub-contract work, it is *your* name that appears on the letterhead and *you* who is responsible for the completed work. If it is poor, then it is you that the client will address any complaint to and you may lose them. One way of making sure is to test the person on work that you receive to do at home and check it before it goes back to the client. This way, you will be able to assess grammar, understanding of the terminology and speed and accuracy with which the work is carried out, measured against your own standards and the standard the client has come to expect.

If the work is good, then you can keep their name on file for future occasions, and you are establishing a link which could lead to successful expansion of your company. This is all very well for home-based work, but what about sub-contracting another freelance to your client's premises? If the freelance is a sole trader or a limited company and they invoice you, then you will not need to change anything in the way your company or accounting system is run.

Acting as a recruitment agent

If you are going to provide someone's services to a company as a representative of your firm, you are in effect acting as an agent yourself. The recruitment agency business is governed by laws requiring the agent to apply for a licence from the Department of Employment. If you are considering becoming an agent for temporary secretaries the whole parameters of your business will need to be changed. It will affect your bookkeeping and you will have to have some knowledge in salaries and wages as you will be paying someone else to work for you. If you are considering expanding your business in this direction, you will need to consult your accountant and to contact the Department of Employment (see your phone book under Employment, Department of, for your local office). Don't forget to negotiate with your clients, if you are unavailable, about you providing interim support via another freelance.

If you decide to turn your business into a recruitment agency, you will also need to become familiar with drawing up advertisements to attract staff to jobs that you might place on your books, or temporary assignments that you currently have vacancies for. You will need to consider the costs of advertising, having someone eight hours a day to answer the telephone, rates to clients and payment of secretaries and what percentage profit you are likely to achieve. You will need enough cash to pay temporary secretaries that work for you on a weekly basis, remembering that you may not get paid by the client until the month end.

'Poaching'

If you simply intend to pass on work to another freelance who will be paid directly by the firm, then it might be a good idea to draw up a very simple agreement in respect of 'poaching'. You do not want to find that you don't hear from either the freelance or the client again because they have renegotiated your price with the client for a lower one and cut you out! It was mentioned under dealing with recruitment agencies that you should never adopt this practice, but it is always best to safeguard your interests by preventing others who may do it to you!

Getting professional advice about sub-contracting

Again, you need not spend a lot of money. Any solicitor will draw up a standard agreement that you can use whenever you feel you need to sub-contract work. If you need a solicitor, contact the Law Society and explain your requirements. They will send you a list of solicitors practising in your area who could handle the type of work you require. As with visiting an accountant, make sure you find out about fees, hourly rates, time that will be required to draw up a contract and an estimate of what a standard form of agreement is likely to cost. The Law Society's address is given in the 'Useful Addresses' at the end of this book.

ADDITIONAL IDEAS

Make a list of the trade magazines for the industry, business or profession that you wish to target; consider how you might advertise your services in them. It may pay to run an advertisement about your secretarial services as a further marketing campaign for achieving work.

- You may want to consider irregular hours typing and offering a 24-hour typing agency. There is demand for this type of service but it s minimal and would not provide you with a satisfactory income on its own.

- Look into ways of varying your service. There are magazines, which are not necessarily directly associated with freelancing secretarial services, through which you might be able to broaden your areas of service. Local libraries, universities and colleges, many institutes and organisations have notice boards. Put a notice up of your service on these boards. It doesn't usually cost anything except the journey and a few drawing pir

- Writers, potential authors, playwrights, all need support

services and quality typing services. The Writers' Guild of Great Britain and the Society of Authors may well be worth approaching to advertise your services.

- Local shops often place cards in their windows for a nominal sum per week. The amount of business you can drum up in this way can be surprising.

- Remember, wherever your service is advertised, the opportunity exists for you to gain a client or make money. There are a lot of ways of advertising which will require little capital outlay, and if you want to expand, then you can invest more money if you feel it is necessary.

RELATED SKILLS

If you start to acquire good systems knowledge, other avenues will open up which you can develop, Some will require advanced training courses, but none the less they are worth consideration. For example:

- systems management

- desk top publishing services

- network management

- database management

- word processing consultancy

- stenography

- language transcription services.

If you decide that you want to specialise, there are a host of courses available which will provide you with a base on which to expand your services. It will be up to you to consider possibilities such as these as and when you feel you are able to expand. As with everything else, the future and what you want to do with it will depend on you.
   Good luck!

10
Questions and Answers

What if the work dries up?
You should never be in this position if you have carried through the continued marketing strategy advocated; if you are continuously approaching companies while you are in work you should be able to secure one lead a month that will result in positive work for you.

How can I limit my start-up costs?
If you do not want to spend the money on becoming a limited company but prefer to test the water you can operate as a sole trader. Ask your local Enterprise Agency about start-up costs and how to minimise expenditure such as this.

While compiling your research and preparing your mailshot lists, you will be able to take on temporary assignments through an agency and win yourself long or short-term bookings. While in assignments through agencies, you can conclude your research and start writing to companies. Equally, if you are in full-time employment, and you wish to start with home-based work in your local area, you can market yourself limiting your marketing to offering typing services. What do you have to lose?

Instead of buying a PC, lease one for a reasonable sum until you are sure that the work you are going to receive warrants purchase. This applies to most equipment available today, and agreements can be made for 'lease purchase'. You will need to consult dealers in the equipment you are interested in who will provide you with information and their terms for lease purchase.

I have never done anything like this before. What if it doesn't work for me?
If you don't try, you won't know and the risks are so minimal that you have little to lose by trying it if you are already a temporary

secretary. If a recession can teach us anything, it is the realisation that security is tenuous in economically difficult times, whether you have a permanent position with a company or not. There is never anything to be lost by trying to work things out for yourself.

What's the best way of doing a mailshot?

To avoid spending money on buying trade and professional directories of companies yourself, your local library will have copies of these.

An up-to-date *Yellow Pages* lists most businesses in the regions. If you do not have a copy for the area you wish to target, one can be obtained from *Yellow Pages* for a nominal sum (£8.00 to £10.00) – see the back of any *Yellow Pages* for details. This should suffice for your initial mailshot.

This established, save yourself time by addressing all your mailshots to the personnel manager, and they will arrive on the right desk.

Use standard white window envelopes for your mailshot. They are cheap, they look presentable and they are easy to use when fitting your letter into them. They avoid the need for labels, which are time-consuming, expensive, laborious and unnecessary. Of course, when setting out your merge letter it is essential to run off a copy of your letter and check the place in which the address will fall first to ensure that you do not end up with a letter which, when folded, does not line up with your window envelope!

A further tip in sending out mailshots is to send them second class on a Friday night. By doing this, they will be on the desk of the addressee by the following Monday: from one business day to the other without the cost of a first-class stamp. Postage costs start to add up when you are sending out batches of two hundred letters at a time – so save yourself some money.

Glossary

Agent	One authorised to or delegated to procure secretarial services to a firm, company, organisation etc.
Agency	A business putting employers and secretaries requiring employment in contact with each other.
Annual turnover	Annual gross income from sales before expenditure has been deducted.
Audit	Examination of the accounts of the company by an authorised person, usually an accountant.
Cashflow forecast	A table forecasting the flow of money in and out of a business – income and expenditure.
Charge rates	Price per hour for secretarial services.
Database	A large body of information conveniently stored in a computer which can process it and from which particular pieces of information can be retrieved when required (eg lists of addresses, details of jobs and invoices).
Dedicated wordprocessor	A computer designed purely for use in conjunction with wordprocessing software.
Desk top publishing	The use of highly advanced software for the production of high standard graphics for letterheads, logos, charts and diagrams and all manner of presentation work.
Disk Operating System (DOS)	The term for the software which enables a computer to function. The best known is MSDOS (Microsoft Disk Operating System).
Disk memory	The room available in a computer's memory for the storage of programs, applications and for the files containing operator work within those programs and applications.

E'Mail	Electronic Mail – information sent via message, letter or memo through a telephone line from one computer to another, anywhere in the world.
Fax box	A box incorporated within a computer to enable facsimile transmissions to an external fax machine.
File (re computing)	Section opened within a directory of a program or application for the storage of data.
Fixed contract	A contract which occurs on a regular basis.
Floppy disk	Usually a 5″ or 3½″ flat media storage cartridge used for inserting into a disk drive on the PC to run off stored data on the hard disk to an external backup.
Freelance	Anyone who works for him/herself, or whose service is paid for by others only for particular, usually short-term assignments.
Hard copy	A copy that is printed out on paper (as opposed to the stored data on the computer).
Hardware	All parts of the PC made with any metals, the cables, the printer, the screen etc.
In-house work	Contracts undertaken by freelances on their own premises.
Invoice	A note of charges for services rendered.
Limited company	A body incorporated in, and subject to, the laws of the United Kingdom for the purposes of accounting. It has its own legal identity, quite separate from the identities of shareholders and directors.
Mailshot letter	A standard letter circulated to many different addresses.
Megabyte	A million times eight digits.
Modem	An electronic device to transmit and receive data.
Mouse	A device with an extensive cable attached to the PC. It is used by the palm of the hand to perform functions within Windows applications. The operator 'clicks on' on the desired on-screen items contained within boxes of lists.
Network	A series of computers either within a firm or universally linked by cables and served by a central processor to enable direct communication.
Package	A program or an application that can be downloaded onto a computer.

PC	Personal computer.
Proforma	A document set up as a standard for repeated use.
Program	A series of hundreds of thousands of commands written in sequence to apply for use with a personal computer.
Scanner	Machine used to capture text or graphics from paper to computer.
Secured creditors	Those first in the queue for payment of monies owed them under the provision of the law when a firm goes into receivership.
Software	All media stored on any form of cartridge (eg hard disk, soft disk, cassette) that can be downloaded onto a computer.
Spreadsheet	Popular form of software specially designed for handling budgets, cashflows and other figure-work.
'State of the art'	The very latest development in something, eg computers.
Systems management	Control and maintenance of a PC, a network, monitoring performance and innovation applications/programs and applications/program aids.
Temp	A temporarily employed secretarial worker – to work as a temp.
Unsecured creditors	Those not guaranteed payment of monies owed them under the provisions of the law when a firm goes into receivership. The last in the queue.
Wordprocessor	A PC used for typing documentation, correspondence, reports etc.
Wordprocessing package	A programme written to specification for the creation and manipulation of text.
Work percentage comparison tables	Tables prepared to compare the different types of work received, the percentages and proportions.

Useful Addresses

GENERAL BUSINESS MATTERS

Business in the Community, 227a City Road, London EC1V. Tel: (071) 253 3716; 5 Cleveland Place, London SW1Y. Tel: (071) 925 2899. This organisation is an umbrella organisation for enterprise agencies in the UK. It has expertise in small business and promoting small business in local communities. The service is free and they are able to provide information on who will be able to assist you in your area. The managers of local Enterprise Agencies are frequently seconded from high levels of management of UK companies and provide a free information service advising on business start-up, cashflow management, marketing and a host of other information.

Confederation of British Industry, 103 New Oxford Street, London WC1A. Tel: (071) 379 7400. This organisation will be able to provide information on reference books to purchase for targeting your business in your area.

Department of Trade & Industry, The Small Firms Service, 1/19 Victoria Street, London SW1H. Tel: (071) 215 5000. This organisation will be able to provide booklets, information and advice on the start-up of a business. The Small Firms Service is a department within the Department of Trade and Industry. It was primarily started to promote small business within local areas and provide books, papers, magazines and staff in local Enterprise Agencies throughout the UK to give free advice to those wishing to start up in business, and being unsure of the procedures that they should follow in terms of finding an accountant, writing cashflows, dealing with banks and all number of bookkeeping matters and general information in regard to running a business. If you are contemplating starting up by yourself and you are not keen to spend money on seeking the advice of an accountant, by contacting the Small Firms Unit they will be able to send you details of local Enterprise Agencies within your area who will be able to assist you. The service is free of charge and well worth the trip.

HM Customs & Excise. Your local office can provide information about all aspects of VAT and how to fill up your VAT returns.

The Inland Revenue. Your local office can help you with leaflets and other information on PAYE and other tax matters.

The Institute of Chartered Accountants in England and Wales, Moorgate Place, London EC2R. Tel: (071) 628 7060. For advice on choosing an accountant.

Institute of Legal Secretaries, ILS House, 76 Denison Road, London SW19 2DH. Tel: (081) 540 0512. This is a relatively new organisation, and provides an information service for legal secretaries in the United Kingdom. They hold conferences, provide information on books and trade magazines and new technology and developments within the legal profession. Their quarterly magazine for members is called *Advocate*. They also run a very useful free Jobs Registry which is distributed throughout subscriber members of the Institute throughout the UK.

The Institute of Wordprocessing, 18 Upper Shirley Road, Shirley, Croydon CR0 5EA. The Institute of Wordprocessing provides its members with new developments in word processing packages, hardware and software and general information on contacts, books and trade developments.

The Law Society, 113 Chancery Lane, London WC2A 1PL. Tel: (071) 242 1222. For advice on choosing a solicitor.

SOFTWARE/HARDWARE HOUSES

It is impossible to list all the UK software houses, but before purchase of a PC, you should phone the relevant manufacturer of the PC you are interested in to find out their authorised dealers within the

UK, and to discuss maintenance contracts and support lines.

Hayes Microcomputer Products Inc., 1 Roundwood Avenue, Stockley Park, Uxbridge, Middlesex UB11 1AE. Tel: (081) 848 1858. Hayes are the leading company in modem development in the UK and if you are considering purchase of a modem, they will be able to supply you with details of their authorised dealers in your region.

MAGAZINES AND REFERENCE BOOKS

Kompass Regional Sales Guide, Reed Information Services Limited, Windsor Court, East Grinstead House, East Grinstead, West Sussex RH19 1XD. Tel: East Grinstead (0342) 326972. Issued annually, this guide produces detailed information and catalogues firms in regional breakdowns in the UK.

The Independent Guide to Secretarial Colleges (1991), Compiled, edited and printed by Angela Mortimer Limited, 37-38 Golden Square, London W1R 9AH. Deals with all available types of secretarial colleges and their courses in the UK. Detailed information on word processing, languages, accounts and business administration.

TRAINING ORGANISATIONS

ICL Training

Mannesmann Keinzle Information Systems Limited, 224 Bath Road, Slough, Berkshire SL1 4DS. Tel: (0753) 33355.

Court reporting or conference transcription skills

Stenography Training College, 126-134 Baker Street, London W1M 1FH. Tel: (071) 935 8242.

Shorthand, word processor, typing and business studies training

Sight & Sound Education Limited, 118-120 Charing Cross Road, London WC2H 0JR. Tel: (071) 377 0301. Sight & Sound also run many regional courses – look in your phone book for your nearest Sight & Sound college and in your local paper for their advertisements.

Pitman, The London Central College, 154 Southampton Row, London WC1B 5AX. Tel: (071) 837 4481.

Speedwriting, 6 Sedley Place, London W1R 1HG. Tel: (071) 586 0084.

Home-learning business courses

Staffordshire Open Learning Unit, The Chetwynd Centre, Newport Road, Stafford ST16 2HE. Tel: (0785) 52313.

STATIONERY AND COMPUTER SUPPLIES BY POST

Action Computer Supplies, Catalogue Distribution Department, 5th Floor, Alperton House, Bridgewater Road, Wembley, Middlesex HA0 1BR. Tel: (0800) 33333.

Neat Ideas Ltd, Freepost, Kirk Sandall, Doncaster DN3 1BR. Tel: (0800) 500192.

FOR ADVERTISING

The Writers' Guild of Great Britain, 430 Edgware Road, London W2 1EH. Tel: (071) 723 8074.

Society of Authors, 84 Drayton Gardens, London SW10 9SB. Tel: (071) 373 6642. Useful for approaching authors for the supply of typing services.

Suggested Reading

RUNNING A BUSINESS

How to Communicate at Work, Ann Dobson (How To Books 1994)
How To Do Your Own Advertising, Michael Bennie (How To Books 1990)
How To Keep Business Accounts, 3rd edition, Peter Taylor (How To Books 1994)
How Manage Budgets & Cashflows, Peter Taylor (How To Books 1994)
How to Manage Computers at Work, Graham Jones (How To Books, 1993)
How to Start a Business From Home, 3rd edition, Graham Jones (How To Books 1994)
How to Work in An Office, Sheila Payne (How To Books 1993)
How to Work From Home, Ian Phillipson (How To Books 1992)

THE WORKING WOMAN

The Working Woman's Guide, L. Hodgkinson (Thorsons 1985)
The Working Woman's Handbook, edited by Audrey Slaughter (Century 1986)

ENGLISH LANGUAGE

Chambers English Dictionary, 7th edition (Chambers 1990)
The Concise Oxford Dictionary, compiled by R. E. Allen (Clarendon Press 1990)
How to Write a Report, John Bowden (How To Books, 2nd edition 1994)
How to Write Business Letters, Ann Dobson (How To Books 1994)

Mind the Stop, 2nd ed, G. V. Carey (Penguin 1958)

Oxford Minidictionary of Spelling, compiled by R. E. Allen (Clarendon Press 1986)

The Penguin Dictionary of Troublesome Words, 2nd edition, Bill Bryson (Penguin 1987)

Mastering English Grammar, S. H. Burton (Macmillan Master Series 1984)

GENERAL

Basic Course Speedwriting (A Wheaton & Co, Exeter 1975)

LEGAL TERMINOLOGY

Legal Thesaurus, William C. Burton (Macmillan Publishing Co. Inc) paperback edition 1985

Index